3

VEGETARIAN
EXPRESS

Also by Nava Atlas

VEGETARIANA

SOUPS FOR ALL SEASONS

AMERICAN HARVEST

VEGETARIAN CELEBRATIONS

Vegetarian EXPRESS

Easy, Tasty, and Healthy Menus in 28 Minutes (or Less!)

Nava Atlas & Lillian Kayte

Illustrations by Nava Atlas

Little, Brown and Company

Boston ◆ New York ◆ Toronto ◆ London

First Edition

Variations on recipes for Peanut Butter Spirals, Cinnamon-Apple Glazed Baby Carrots, Tofu Migas, Corn-Olive Salad, Aztec Platter, Baked Bananas, Pineapple Ambrosia, and Baked Pears first appeared in *Vegetarian Times* magazine in articles by Nava Atlas.

Variations on recipes for Warm and Hearty Two-Rice Salad, Vegetable Lo Mein, New York Reuben Pizza, and Spicy Black Bean Burgers first appeared in *Vegetarian Times* magazine in articles by Lillian Kayte.

TVP® (used in recipes for Easy TVP Chili and TVP Sloppy Joes) is a registered trademark of the Archer Daniels Midland Corporation, Decatur, IL.

Library of Congress Cataloging-in-Publication Data

Atlas, Nava.
     Vegetarian express: easy, tasty, and healthy menus in 28 minutes or less /
Nava Atlas and Lillian Kayte; illustrations by Nava Atlas. — 1st ed.
        p.   cm.
     Includes index.
     ISBN 0-316-05740-1
     1. Vegetarian cookery.   2. Cookery (Natural foods)   3. Quick and easy
     cookery.   4. Menus.   I. Kayte, Lillian.   II. Title.
TX837.A853 1995
641.5'636 — dc20

10 9 8 7 6 5 4

MV-NY

Published simultaneously in Canada by Little, Brown & Company (Canada) Limited

Printed in the United States of America

For Chaim, at long last
— N. A.

For Sophie Kayte, who set the standard
and passed the wonder on
— L. K.

Contents

PREFACE

Meatless Meals in 28 Minutes or Less: It *Can* Be Done!

Everyone wants to eat healthfully and well, but, too often, time crunched people believe that a steady diet of great, home-cooked meals is simply not a possibility for them. This book will prove that you don't need a lot of time or planning to serve meals that are tasty, healthy, and satisfying — even exotic and fun.

High-quality meals need not be sacrificed to a fast-paced life. Spending a couple of hours — or even a single hour — in the kitchen at the tag end of a nine-to-five day (or as is often the case, even longer days for those with demanding careers or those who juggle work and family responsibilities) is unrealistic as well as unappealing. However, with a pantry stocked with convenient natural foods, plus a little ingenuity, anyone can prepare terrific meals in 28 minutes or less — no more time than it will take to eat them.

Granted, even busy people can and do find the time now and again to make a long-simmering soup or stew, a complex casserole, and other dishes that take a bit more time. But if you're one of the type of people who often find themselves in the kitchen at 5:30 or 6:00 (or later!) in a panic over what to make for dinner, we trust that among these menus you will discover your own favorite repertoire of meals that will please you and your family each and every day.

With the help of this book, you will have more than seventy-five menus to choose from for those busy days, instead of the usual two — pizza or Chinese takeout!

Our quick and tasty menus are all meatless, but we've designed them so that they appeal not just to vegetarians but also to others:

- Those who would like to add more vegetarian and ethnic meals to their repertoire but are still under the impression that this style of cooking is too time-consuming.

- People who would like to add more beans and grains to their diet and are under the similar impression that these foods are too time-consuming to prepare. Our recipes, which utilize quick-cooking grains and canned beans, will dispel this misconception.

- College students who cook for themselves.

- People who keep promising themselves to eat healthier, lower-fat meals but never do so because they don't have time to think about it, let alone plan for it.

- Families with young children. We know from experience how rare it is to get even thirty minutes alone in the kitchen.

Within this range of menus, you'll find everything from the most simple of meals and family-style favorites to the fairly sophisticated and somewhat exotic. Our highly organized, step-by-step menus should be a boon to the beginning cook, though we would hope that these meals will appeal to more experienced cooks as well — everyone needs to make meals in a hurry at least once in a while, and for the latter, this collection will serve as a fresh cache of ideas.

Most recipes here rely on ingredients found at any supermarket, while several will require a trip to a natural food store. There's something to suit every taste here, and we've grouped the menus so that you can find what you're in the mood for quickly and easily.

These menus were designed by two women with completely different backgrounds but with a similar outlook and similar situations at particular times in our lives that led us to need and appreciate a quick-cooking repertoire.

AUTHORS' NOTES

Lillian Kayte

Despite the fact that my mother was an amazing cook, she wasn't willing to suffer fools in her kitchen. As a result, I hadn't learned how to cook by the time I married. Nevertheless, I planned my first dinner party a week after returning from my honeymoon. I remember the elaborate menu, the shopping, setting the table with damask, crystal, and candles, putting on my best basic black, pearls, and high heels, and going into the kitchen. The rest is a humiliating blur.

That was back in the fifties, and a lot of dinner parties have come from my kitchen since then, which I can only attribute to the hope that springs eternal in the human breast. Ultimately, I became almost as good a cook as my mother. She had set the standard; I followed.

I became a mother, too, then a working mother, then a stepmother to an even larger family. By then it was the late sixties, and I had become adept in the kitchen, putting cooked-from-scratch meals on the table for eight people every night after a day at the office, often preparing them in a half hour or less. Though the meals I cooked back then weren't meatless, I always aimed for wholesomeness. You'll find many of the strategies I used then in the pages of this book.

My real appreciation for food and its preparation didn't begin until 1974, when I lived in Nice. Armed with Julia Child's *Mastering the Art of French Cooking,* I began spending time in the kitchens of my French friends; at the local Lycee Technique, where I could dip into the courses they gave in restaurant cuisine; at the small neighborhood shops; and at the big open market where I went each day to buy fresh produce. I made friends, listened, watched, asked endless questions, and learned.

The French passion for food and its preparation was contagious. I became as zealous as they, demanding the best that the markets had to offer. When we returned to the States, I was invited to teach French cuisine through the local university, then began teaching area chefs as well. I started writing for magazines and newspapers in 1977, worked as a food and lifestyle editor for a succession of daily newspapers, became a vegetarian in 1991, and then settled down to write exclusively about vegetarian cooking.

Contrary to popular belief, vegetarian dishes can often be less cumbersome and time-consuming to prepare than dishes involving meat, and they lend themselves well to quick-cooking techniques. Even though my family is grown and gone now, this type of cooking still best suits my schedule.

Appreciating food doesn't involve time as much as it does awareness. The nutty aromas of whole grains, the delicate fragrance of fresh herbs, the flavor of a perfect sun-ripened tomato all awaken the senses. As you handle the grains, beans, vegetables, and fruits called for in our menus, open yourself to the wonder of it — and pass the wonder on.

Nava Atlas

As with Lillian, the appreciation of food and cooking, specifically vegetarian cooking, is a deeply ingrained part of my life. But though Lillian and I have come to have remarkably similar tastes and philosophies about food, the context in which this meeting of minds occurred was radically different.

While Lillian was busy working and raising her large family, I was growing up, a child of the sixties, in training to be a rebellious teenager. In fact, I became a vegetarian while in my teens, and my eating habits were part of that rebellion and reflected the tumultuous era in which I grew up.

Figuring that my giving up meat was just another phase, my parents said that I would have to cook for myself if I wanted vegetarian meals. This strategy backfired, though, as I quickly realized that I adored cooking. And ironically, not only did I discover a lifelong passion for vegetarian cookery, but also my parents and my two older brothers all gradually gave up meat for good.

The man who became my husband had no qualms about my dietary preferences; in fact, he was quite eager to become a vegetarian. No cook himself, he relished our home-cooked dinners — so much that he urged me to write down my recipes, some of which were my own concoctions, while others were simplified versions of meals we enjoyed at the ethnic restaurants of New York City, where we lived when we were first married.

Eventually, the recipes I compiled became my first book, *Vegetariana: A Rich Harvest of Wit, Lore, and Recipes,* published in 1984. Since then, I have written and illustrated several other of my own vegetarian cookbooks, all created with the luxury of time to experiment, research, and travel.

By now this story seems like ancient history, B.C. — Before Children, that is. After having two sons in quick succession, preparing a decent dinner suddenly seemed as monumental a task as climbing Mount Everest. Being a cookbook author was irrelevant to my new role as overwhelmed mother, and my husband's marginal kitchen skills were of little help. During that crazed first year, my husband and I subsisted on catch-as-catch-can meals, plus a lot of take-out food. Always used to eating well, we sorely missed our colorful, tasty meals.

What I considered simple meals in the days "B.C." didn't seem simple enough for the situation at hand, so I began to develop a repertoire of very efficient, pared-down versions of the kinds of meals we liked best. Soon I was able to make a decent dinner once again, but now usually in fewer than twenty-five minutes.

As I write this, my babies are now young boys, and life is easier. But these menus are still my constant companions. I don't mind having to make a separate meal for my finicky vegetarian boys — as I often do — if preparing a fresh and flavorful meal that my husband and I can thoroughly enjoy takes only twenty-eight minutes or less.

All too often, good food, the enjoyment of it, and as Lillian points out, the appreciation of it, fall by the wayside during the throes of a fast-paced life. Enjoying a tasty, nourishing meal at the end of the day is practically essential to my well-being, and I would have hated to let that go. These menus have helped me preserve that part of my lifestyle, even as I raise young children and continue my work as a writer and designer. If this book helps others with time-crunched lives eat better, feel healthier, and actually enjoy preparing meals, that would gratify me immensely.

VEGETARIAN EXPRESS

INTRODUCTION

How to Use These Menus

We promise you wholesome, tasty meals in twenty-eight minutes or less. While we were as diligent as could be about timing our preparation, and even included a "fudge factor," prep time can be a bit subjective. Our time frame entails working at an unhurried yet steady pace. Interruptions such as diapering a baby, chatting with a delivery person, or answering a phone call are not factored in! Here are a few tips to help you complete these menus successfully and in the allotted time:

- Check our handy ingredient lists on the sidebar of each menu. These will let you easily determine if you have all the items you need for a certain meal. If not, you can jot down any missing ingredients and fresh foods to pick up during the course of your day.

- Before starting, group together on your counter all the ingredients needed for each recipe in a menu. Going back and forth many times from your workspace to your cabinets and from your workspace to your refrigerator in search of ingredients is a big time waster.

- Just before beginning to cook, look over our strategy list. Think of this as the "time management" portion of the preparation. It will tell you in simple terms how to juggle the preparation of the components of the menu so that every valuable minute is well spent.

- If you find yourself pushing the twenty-eight-minute time limit the first time you tackle a menu (although we hope this will not happen), don't be discouraged. Once you become more familiar with ingredients and procedures that may be new to you, you will become more adept and may even find yourself beating our allotted prep time.

We've often heard busy people complain that when they feel frazzled, they just don't know what they are in the mood to eat. We've helped solve this dilemma, too, by arranging the menus thematically, for example, pasta meals, Mexican-style meals, sandwiches, salad meals, and so on. Further, you'll find a list of menus at the beginning of each chapter that can be quickly scanned, making your choice even easier.

Finally, there is an additional bonus to the type of streamlined cooking you'll find here: because the cooking procedures are kept simple, you'll also find that cleanup is easy. After all, what good is a simple meal if you have to spend hours cleaning up afterward?

Convenient Ingredients at the Heart of Quick Meals

For busy people, the notion of cooking *everything* from scratch, for all meals, is a complete fantasy. And while everyone would admit that cooked-from-scratch meals are the most whole-some and appealing, most would agree that making such meals is simply not an option when one is caught in the throes of a hectic life.

While we feature many wholesome foods in our menus, including fresh fruits and veg-etables, grains, beans, pasta, and soy foods, many of these are used in their most convenient forms. At the heart of these menus, which will allow even the busiest of people to eat well every day, is a core group of ingredients we call convenient foods.

Convenient foods aren't the same as *convenience* foods, which are already prepared and need only be heated up (like frozen pizza, frozen egg rolls, ready-made veggie burgers, or the like). While products such as these can also be a boon on busy days, you certainly don't need a cookbook to tell you how to use them.

Our most frequently used convenient foods are products such as canned beans, quick-cooking grains, and certain frozen or good-quality canned items whose use would otherwise be impossible in meals that are needed in a hurry. We also consider pasta, tofu, and ready-to-use fresh vegetables like precut coleslaw cabbage, baby carrots, and precut broccoli florets conve-nient foods because they demand so little of the cook's time or effort.

In preparing the following list of pantry, refrigerator, and freezer staples, we recognize that what is a staple to one cook may be an oddity to another. With that in mind, we have tried to keep these lists as general as could be within the framework of our menus. If you would like to try a number of these menus or, in general, enjoy a quick style of healthy, meatless cooking more often, this list will help you organize your shopping habits so that you have many essential ingredients on hand at all times.

Pantry Staples

Beans, canned (these are frequently used in our menus, so we recommend keeping several
varieties, in 1-pound cans, on hand)
    Black or turtle beans
    Chickpeas (garbanzos)
    Great Northern beans (cannellini)
    Pink beans
    Pinto beans
    Red or kidney beans
Chilies, green, in 4-ounce cans, chopped, mild to hot as preferred
Cornstarch
Flour, unbleached (for thickening)
Grains
    Quick-cooking brown rice
    Specialty grains (those used in our menus are couscous, quinoa, kasha, and bulgur; these
    are, however, listed in the shopping lists, since we recognize that not everyone considers
    these grains staples)
Herbs and spices, dried (keep a good range of commonly used varieties on hand; seasoning
    blends, especially an all-purpose salt-free herb-and-spice blend, as well as an Italian herb
    seasoning blend, are especially useful)
Oils
    Canola oil (we recommend this as an all-purpose cooking oil, since it has an excellent
    profile of polyunsaturated fats; however, safflower oil is also a very good choice)
    Dark sesame oil
    Extra-virgin olive oil
    Light olive oil
    Vegetable oil or olive oil cooking spray
Olives, black pitted, 8-ounce or 1-pound cans
Onions
Pastas
    Keep a good supply of different sizes and shapes of pasta in your pantry at all times. Some that
    are used frequently in our menus include angel hair or cappellini, vermicelli or thin spaghetti,
    spirals, also called rotelle or rotini, ziti or penne, fettuccine, and linguine. A few recipes call for
    Oriental noodles such as udon or soba, available in natural food stores (in whole-grain form)
    or Oriental groceries. However, spaghetti and linguine are recommended as substitutes.
    Though definitely a pantry staple, we often list the particular type of pasta needed in a menu
    in the shopping list, since you may not necessarily have it on hand at any given time.

Peanut butter
Raisins, dark
Soy sauce (sometimes marketed under the terms tamari or shoyu; buy a good-quality brand
    for best flavor)
Sweeteners
    Brown-rice syrup (recommended as a substitute for honey)
    Granulated sugar
    Honey
    Light and dark brown sugars
Tomato paste
Tomatoes, canned
    Crushed or pureed, in 14-ounce and 28-ounce cans
    Whole plum tomatoes, in 14-ounce cans
Vinegars
    Apple cider vinegar
    Red-wine vinegar
    White-wine or rice vinegar
Wine, dry red and white, and cooking sherry

Refrigerator Staples

Refrigerator staples are even more subjective to define than pantry staples. We imagine that each and every cook has a definite idea of what are staples in their refrigerator. That being the case, we present a fairly short and simple list, concentrating on the ingredients that are constant essentials in our menus. Other items that may be staples for many of you (certain perishable cheeses and fresh fruits and vegetables, or even tofu), we have left to our shopping lists for individual menus to serve as a checklist for everyone's convenience.

Butter or soy margarine (both of these are used quite sparingly; we recommend soy marga-
    rine purchased from natural food stores, as it is the most natural in terms of ingredients
    and the least problematic in terms of the transfatty acids controversy)
Carrots, fresh
Celery, fresh
Eggs or egg substitute (these are very infrequently called for in our menus, so they need not
    concern anyone who doesn't use them)
Garlic, fresh

Grated Parmesan cheese (preferably freshly grated and bought by weight from a specialty
    food shop, or you can keep a hard chunk in your refrigerator, which keeps well if care-
    fully wrapped, and grate the amount needed for each use)
Ketchup
Lemons
Margarine, see Butter or soy margarine
Mayonnaise, reduced-fat, or commercially prepared tofu mayonnaise
Milk, low-fat, or soy milk
Mustard, prepared
    Dijon-style
    Grainy dark
Olives, green, pimiento-stuffed
Salad dressings
    Italian, low-fat
    Red-wine vinegar and oil, low-fat
Sour cream, reduced-fat
Wheat germ, toasted, plain
Yogurt, plain

Freezer Staples

This is a very basic list of frozen items most frequently used in our menus.

Apple juice concentrate
Corn kernels, 10-ounce boxes or 1-pound bag
Green peas, 10-ounce boxes or 1-pound bag
Orange juice concentrate
Spinach, 10-ounce boxes
Tortillas, corn, 1 dozen
Tortillas, wheat, 1 dozen

Time-Saving Tips and Techniques

- To get cloves of garlic to release their skin more easily, crush the clove slightly with the flat side of a chef's knife.

- Though a steamer basket is a useful kitchen gadget, you don't necessarily need one to steam vegetables successfully. You'll get good results with most vegetables by placing them in a deep saucepan with a half-inch to an inch of water (depending on the volume of vegetables) and cooking, covered, over medium-high heat.

- Sautéing goes more quickly if you use a cover. This saves time when sautéing onions, bell peppers, and other vegetables.

- Similarly, a pot of water will come to a boil somewhat more quickly if you cover it. This is useful when you are bringing a big pot of water to a boil for pasta.

- And speaking of pasta, be sure to cook it at a steady (but not frantic) boil at all times for best, and quickest, results.

- When chopping parsley, do as professional chefs do: keep the bunch tied together and thinly slice what you need from the top, tender stems and all. This by far beats tediously separating leaves from the stems. Store the parsley in a jar of water, stems down, and cover lightly with a plastic bag. Refrigerate, and change the water daily.

- Make a quick task of thawing frozen vegetables by first placing them in a colander, then running warm water through them until they separate and any ice particles have melted. Then cook or microwave briefly, depending on the variety of vegetable.

- Don't make a whole production of chopping onions. Unless a recipe calls for finely chopped onion (which ours rarely do), the quickest route to a chopped onion is by simply quartering and slicing it.

- If you need several carrots or celery stalks sliced, lay three or four side by side on a cutting board and slice them at the same time with a good, sharp knife.

Explanation of Nutritional Analysis

All breakdowns are based on one serving, unless specified otherwise. When there's a range in the serving amount, the average number of servings is used (i.e., when a recipe specifies 6 to 8 servings, the analysis is based on 7 servings).

When more than one ingredient is listed as an option (i.e., soy margarine or butter), the first ingredient is used in the analysis. Usually, the option ingredient will not change the analysis significantly. Ingredients listed as optional, most often found at the end of the recipe, however, are not included in the analysis.

When salt is listed "to taste," its sodium content is not included in the analysis.

Useful Equipment

These menus were designed for kitchens that are equipped in a fairly basic way. There are a few tools that we would consider, if not essential, at least very useful for anyone who is serious about quick cooking.

Microwave oven: Though none of our menus are dependent on microwaves (except where we recommend baked potatoes or sweet potatoes as a side dish), they do come in handy for quickly cooking or thawing frozen vegetables, warming tortillas and other breads, and the like. But we can freely say that you need not own a microwave oven to fully use these menus.

Food processor: The food processor is another matter. We feel this tool is really necessary for anyone who is serious about preparing quick meals often. While you can make most of these meals without a food processor, we do call for its use far more than we do a microwave. It's essential for replacing laborious hand grating. Food processors are also handy for pureeing dressings and instant sauces or puddings, and for finely chopping nuts, vegetables, and herbs.

Good-quality knives: A good knife can really make the difference in chopping and dicing, making these tasks a breeze instead of a big project.

Nonstick cookware in a variety of sizes: Good-quality nonstick cookware is probably the most important investment to make for your kitchen. You'll use less fat in cooking, and cleanup time will also be cut. For our menus, you'll need only what comes in a basic set — a soup pot, a large and a small saucepan, and a large, a medium-sized, and a small skillet, all with matching lids. A good nonstick wok can also come in handy for stir-fries and for one-dish meals of hefty quantity.

Chapter One

QUICK! COOK THE NOODLES!

This chapter is named for Nava's idea of meal planning during those truly frantic days when both her sons were babies. She would rush into the kitchen at five-thirty in the afternoon, with only this thought going through her head: "Quick! Cook the noodles!"

We would bet that many cooks have similar thoughts when they want dinner in a hurry. Pasta is the perfect quick food — most varieties cook quickly enough to accommodate ravenous hunger, yet allow enough cooking time to prepare a simple sauce and a salad, with perhaps time to spare to cut some bread. It's hard not to love pasta, and wonder of wonders, even kids will eat it (even if you have to leave the sauce *you* like off their portion and just add a little butter or cheese to please finicky tastes).

For those who frequently find themselves in the kitchen thinking "Quick! Cook the noodles!" two must-haves are a pantry well stocked with many varieties of pasta, and a repertoire of quick menus ranging from basic to sophisticated. You'll have to take care of the pantry part; we'll help you do the rest.

Ziti with Broccoli in Garlic Sauce
Artichoke and White Bean Dip with Crudités
Hot dinner rolls

Indonesian Noodles
Sweet-Glazed Tofu Cutlets
Kirby cucumber spears

Bowtie Pasta with Artichokes and Mushrooms
Crostini with Sun-Dried Tomato Pesto
Simple tossed salad

Pennsylvania Dutch Corn Noodles
Dutch-Style Sweet-and-Sour Slaw
Steamed green beans or zucchini
Fresh rye bread

Angel Hair Pasta with Pine Nuts and Sun-Dried Tomatoes
Italian Chopped Salad
Steamed broccoli
Broiled garlic toast

Peanut Butter Spirals
Cinnamon-Apple Glazed Baby Carrots
Sliced cucumbers, celery sticks, and tomatoes

Fettuccine in Green Chili Corn Sauce
Deviled Tomatoes
Fat-free tortilla chips
Carrot and jicama sticks

Vegetable Lo Mein
Gratin of Beets and Walnuts
Carrot and celery sticks

Vermicelli with Fresh Tomato and Basil Sauce
Mozzarella slices with black olives
Corn-on-the-cob

Rotini with Spinach, Chickpeas, and Sun-Dried Tomatoes
Carrot and Raisin Salad
Fresh bread of your choice

Fettuccine with Pesto Florentine
Italian Herbed Bread
Tossed green salad

Simple Sesame-Soy Oriental Noodles
Broccoli, Carrot, and Cashew Stir-Fry with Tofu

Pasta Puttanesca
Gorgonzola-Lettuce Wedges
Warm kaiser rolls

Pasta with Garlic and Oil
Baked Breaded Zucchini, Mushrooms, and Tofu
Cherry tomatoes and sliced bell peppers

Pasta Mexicana
Hot corn bread or corn muffins (purchased)
Tossed greens with cucumbers, broccoli florets, and olives

Curried Pasta with Ricotta, Red Onion, Peas, and Raisins
Tossed salad
Chapatis or other flatbread

_____ *MENU* _____

Ziti with Broccoli in Garlic Sauce

**Artichoke and White Bean Dip
with Crudités**

Hot dinner rolls

Serves 4 to 6

_____

If you want children to grow up to have an eclectic, adventurous attitude toward food, start them off early with a pasta dinner like this one. It's perfect for every age group because it's easy to digest, high in fiber, and low in saturated fats and cholesterol. What more can you ask from a simple meal that's fit for a king?

_____

Strategy:

1. Cook the pasta. While it cooks, prepare the artichoke dip. Cut raw vegetables for crudités.

2. Cut and steam the broccoli stems and florets according to the recipe directions.

3. Continue the pasta recipe from step 3 to the end.

ZITI WITH BROCCOLI IN GARLIC SAUCE

Adults might like the spicy kick of a bit of jalapeño pepper; leave it out if you're serving this dish to kids.

10 to 12 ounces ziti or penne pasta
⅓ cup low-fat milk or soy milk
1 large bunch fresh broccoli, or about 4 heaping cups precut fresh broccoli florets
¼ cup olive oil
4 large cloves garlic, minced
1 small jalepeño pepper, minced (optional)
⅓ cup grated Parmesan cheese or soy Parmesan
Salt and freshly ground pepper, to taste

1. Bring a large pot of water to a boil and cook the pasta at a steady simmer until *al dente*. When the pasta is done, drain it, return it to the pot, and toss it with milk or soy milk. Remove the pasta pot from the heat and cover.

2. In the meantime, if using a bunch of broccoli, cut the stalks away from the florets, then trim and peel them. Cut the stalks crosswise into ¼-inch slices and cut the florets into pieces about 1 inch in diameter. Steam the cut broccoli or precut florets in a saucepan with about an inch of water for about 5 minutes, or until they're bright green and tender-crisp.

3. Heat the oil in a small skillet. Add the garlic and the jalapeño pepper, if desired. Sauté them over low heat for 1 minute, then mash them into the oil with a fork and continue to sauté over very low heat for 2 minutes.

4. Add the steamed broccoli and the garlic mixture to the pasta in the pot. Add the Parmesan cheese, season to taste with salt and pepper, and serve.

Calories: 217	Total fat: 11 g	Protein: 6 g
Carbohydrate: 19 g	Cholesterol: 5 g	Sodium: 146 mg

ARTICHOKE AND WHITE BEAN DIP WITH CRUDITÉS

Use as a spread for toast, as a sauce over hot freshly cooked pasta, or, as we have done, as a dip for crispy crudités.

14-ounce can artichoke hearts, drained, reserving the juice
1-pound can white beans, drained and rinsed
2 scallions, chopped
½ teaspoon dried thyme leaves
Several grinds of black pepper
Salt, to taste (optional)
Assorted fresh crisp vegetables for dipping: carrot and celery sticks, red bell pepper wedges, scallions, etc.

1. Combine the artichokes, white beans, scallions, and thyme in a food processor fitted with a steel blade; puree. Add the artichoke juice in dribbles as necessary until the dip is of a medium-thick consistency.

2. Transfer the puree to a small serving bowl. Add pepper and a pinch of salt, if desired. Put the bowl on a plate and surround it with the cut vegetables.

Calories: 155	Total fat: 0 g	Protein: 9 g
Carbohydrate: 29 g	Cholesterol: 0 g	Sodium: 43 mg

Pantry staples
- ❏ Olive oil
- ❏ Dried thyme
- ❏ Great Northern beans or cannellini, 1-pound can
- ❏ Ziti or penne pasta
- ❏ Fresh garlic

Refrigerator staples
- ❏ Low-fat milk or soy milk
- ❏ Parmesan or soy Parmesan cheese

Shopping list: fresh foods and nonstaples
- ❏ Fresh broccoli or fresh precut broccoli florets, about 1½ pounds
- ❏ Fresh vegetables for crudités: carrots, celery or celery hearts, red bell peppers, or other crisp vegetables of your choice
- ❏ Fresh jalepeño pepper (optional)
- ❏ Artichoke hearts, 14-ounce can
- ❏ Scallions, 1 bunch
- ❏ Dinner rolls

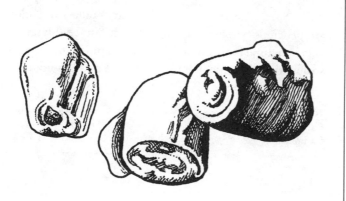

MENU

Indonesian Noodles

Sweet-Glazed Tofu Cutlets

Kirby cucumber spears

Serves 4

The Oriental traditions have introduced us to numerous delicious ways to serve noodles, many quite simple. Here is the first of several menus throughout this book that feature tasty Asian noodle dishes. Using imported noodles lends an authentic touch; these noodles are widely available in natural food markets. We encourage you to try them, but if you're the least bit intimidated, go ahead and use the substitutions recommended in the recipes.

Strategy:

1. Begin cooking the noodles.

2. While the water is coming to a boil, begin preparing the tofu dish and continue until the tofu is in the skillet frying.

3. Continue with the noodle recipe from step 2 on.

4. Remove the tofu dish from the heat when it's done and garnish.

INDONESIAN NOODLES

½ pound soba or udon noodles (see Note)
2 tablespoons peanut oil or other vegetable oil
1 large onion, quartered and thinly sliced
3 cloves garlic, minced
1 teaspoon grated fresh ginger, or ¼ teaspoon ground ginger
½ pound fresh mung bean sprouts
1 to 1½ cups snow peas, trimmed
2 tablespoons soy sauce, or to taste
Hot red-pepper flakes, to taste (optional)
Dry-roasted peanuts for garnish

1. Begin cooking the noodles.

2. Heat the oil in a wok or very large skillet. Add the onion and garlic and sauté over moderate heat until the onion is golden, about 5 minutes.

3. Add the remaining ingredients except the peanuts and stir-fry over moderately high heat until the sprouts and snow peas are tender-crisp, about 5 minutes more.

4. When the noodles are done, drain them, add them to the wok, and continue to stir-fry for another 3 to 4 minutes. Remove the noodles from the heat and serve, garnishing each serving with a scattering of peanuts.

Note: Soba (also known as buckwheat noodles) and udon are delicious whole-grain noodles that are readily available in natural food stores. If you're in a pinch, use regular spaghetti or linguine; the results will be good though not quite as interesting.

Calories: 194	Total fat: 6 g	Protein: 6 g
Carbohydrate: 25 g	Cholesterol: 0 g	Sodium: 513 mg

SWEET-GLAZED TOFU CUTLETS

We would challenge anyone who thinks that tofu is tasteless mush to try this simple recipe. Crisp and salty-sweet, tofu is rarely better than this.

1 pound firm tofu, drained
1 tablespoon safflower or canola oil
1 teaspoon sesame oil
2 tablespoons honey or brown rice syrup
2 tablespoons soy sauce
2 tablespoons dry red wine or sherry
2 scallions, sliced, for garnish

1. Cut the tofu crosswise into ¼-inch-thick slices. Blot the slices briefly between paper towels or clean tea towels.

2. Combine the oils, honey or rice syrup, soy sauce, and wine or sherry in a small bowl, then heat the mixture slowly in a wide skillet.

3. Arrange the tofu slices in the skillet, then flip them carefully at once so that they will be coated with the sauce on both sides. Fry the tofu over moderately high heat until the underside is nicely golden and crisp, then flip again and fry until the other side is crisp.

4. Remove the tofu cutlets to a serving platter and scatter with scallion slices.

Calories: 170	Total fat: 9 g	Protein: 8 g
Carbohydrate: 11 g	Cholesterol: 0 g	Sodium: 513 mg

Strategy, continued

5. While the two dishes cook, scrub and slice several small Kirby cucumbers into spears and arrange them on a plate.

Pantry staples
❑ Safflower or canola oil
❑ Dark sesame oil
❑ Peanut oil or other vegetable oil
❑ Honey or brown rice syrup
❑ Soy sauce
❑ Onion, 1 large
❑ Dry red wine or sherry
❑ Hot red-pepper flakes

Refrigerator staples
❑ Fresh garlic

Shopping list: fresh foods and nonstaples
❑ Fresh mung bean sprouts, 8-ounce package
❑ Fresh snow peas, about ¼ pound
❑ Firm tofu, 1 pound
❑ Fresh ginger
❑ Scallions, 1 bunch
❑ Kirby cucumbers, 3 or 4
❑ Soba or udon noodles (substitute spaghetti or linguine if necessary), ½-pound package
❑ Dry-roasted peanuts

MENU

Bowtie Pasta with Artichokes and Mushrooms

Crostini with Sun-Dried Tomato Pesto

Simple tossed salad

Serves 6 to 8

No matter what your ancestral heritage, this is the kind of comfort food everyone relates to. A northern Italian-inspired dish of pasta, artichokes, and mushrooms in a creamy sauce, served with crostini (toast) spread with a rich, thick, sun-dried tomato pesto, is a winning combination that might well become a permanent fixture in your repertoire.

Strategy:

1. Preheat the oven to 350 degrees.

2. Begin cooking the pasta. While it cooks, prepare the artichoke and mushroom sauce.

3. In a food processor fitted with a steel blade, blend the ingredients for the tomato pesto and set aside.

4. Place the bread in the oven to start toasting, then turn it and remove as directed in the recipe.

5. Do the last step of the pesto recipe.

BOWTIE PASTA WITH ARTICHOKES AND MUSHROOMS

10 to 12 ounces bowtie (farfalle) pasta
8 ounces white mushrooms, wiped clean and
    cut into quarters
10-ounce package frozen artichoke hearts,
    or 14-ounce can artichoke hearts, drained
    (reserve liquid) and quartered
8 ounces soft, low-fat cream cheese (Neufchâtel)
2 tablespoons lemon juice
Freshly ground pepper, to taste
¼ cup grated Parmesan cheese
⅓ cup toasted wheat germ
¼ cup chopped fresh parsley, or more or less to taste

1. Cook the pasta in rapidly simmering water until *al dente*.

2. While the pasta cooks, spray a large skillet with cooking oil spray and place it over high heat. Add ¼ cup water and "sweat" the mushrooms, covered, for 2 or 3 minutes, or until slightly wilted. Add the artichoke hearts and continue cooking, uncovered, until most of the liquid is gone, about 3 minutes more.

3. Cut the Neufchâtel cheese into several pieces and add them to the skillet with 1 cup of water or the reserved liquid from the canned artichokes plus enough water to make 1 cup. With a wooden spoon, gently smooth the sauce while it comes to a simmer. Add the lemon juice and pepper, plus any additional water, if needed, to bring the sauce to a medium consistency.

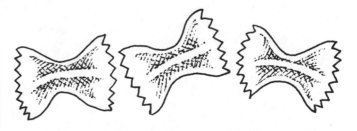

4. When the pasta is done, drain it, then combine it in a large serving bowl with the sauce and mix well. Sprinkle the pasta with the Parmesan cheese, then the wheat germ and parsley, and serve immediately.

| Calories: 200 | Total fat: 9 g | Protein: 9 g |
| Carbohydrate: 19 g | Cholesterol: 31 g | Sodium: 207 mg |

CROSTINI WITH SUN-DRIED TOMATO PESTO

1 loaf French or Italian bread
Olive oil cooking spray
4 ounces oil-cured sun-dried tomatoes
1 medium bunch fresh basil (remove thick stems, but don't be fussy about small ones)
1 large clove garlic, chopped
2 tablespoons grated Parmesan cheese, preferably fresh
3 tablespoons walnuts

1. Preheat the oven to 350 degrees. Slice the bread into ½-inch diagonal slices, spray lightly on both sides with olive oil, and toast until dry and crisp, about 5 to 7 minutes.

2. Drain the sun-dried tomatoes (reserve the oil for another use, such as for salad dressing or sautéing), then place them along with the remaining ingredients in a food processor fitted with a steel blade. Process, using brief on/off pulses, until the mixture is evenly ground but with a little texture remaining.

3. Scoop the pesto into a crock or bowl, put it in the center of a plate, and surround with the crostini.

| Calories: 236 | Total fat: 8 g | Protein: 8 g |
| Carbohydrate: 31 g | Cholesterol: 1 g | Sodium: 284 mg |

Strategy, continued

6. Complete the pasta recipe.

7. At odd moments during the preparation of the meal, prepare a simple tossed salad. A combination of dark green lettuce leaves, tomatoes, raw broccoli florets, and carrots complements this meal well. Dress as desired.

Pantry staples
❏ Olive oil cooking spray

Refrigerator staples
❏ Fresh garlic
❏ Toasted wheat germ
❏ Lemon, 1
❏ Grated Parmesan cheese

Shopping list: fresh foods and nonstaples
❏ Soft, low-fat cream cheese (Neufchâtel), 8-ounce package
❏ White mushrooms, 8 ounces
❏ Fresh basil, 1 bunch
❏ Fresh parsley, 1 bunch
❏ French or Italian bread, 1 long loaf
❏ Bowtie pasta (farfalle), 1-pound package
❏ Frozen artichoke hearts, 10-ounce package, or canned artichoke hearts, 14-ounce can
❏ Sun-dried tomatoes, oil-cured, 4 ounces
❏ Walnuts, shelled
❏ Salad vegetables of choice or as suggested in strategy list

MENU

Pennsylvania Dutch Corn Noodles

Dutch-Style Sweet-and-Sour Slaw

Steamed green beans or zucchini

Fresh rye bread

Serves 6

The Pennsylvania Dutch tradition cherishes the "plain and simple" in all ways of living, culinary arts included. But "plain and simple" need not mean "boring and bland." In this case, it means filling, flavorful, and simple to prepare.

Strategy:

1. Begin cooking the noodles.

2. While the water is coming to a boil, prepare the slaw recipe.

3. Cook the noodles, and in the meantime proceed with the recipe for the corn noodles.

4. While the noodles are cooking and the skillet mixture is simmering, steam about ½ pound of trimmed fresh green beans, or 2 medium zucchini, cut into 2-inch spears.

PENNSYLVANIA DUTCH CORN NOODLES

½ pound yolk-free ribbon egg noodles
2 tablespoons soy margarine
1 large onion, quartered and thinly sliced
1-pound bag frozen succotash (mixed corn and lima beans), thawed
1½ pounds fresh tomatoes, diced, plus ¼ cup water (or substitute a 28-ounce can plum tomatoes, chopped, with liquid)
¼ cup chopped fresh parsley
Salt and freshly ground pepper, to taste

1. Begin cooking the noodles.

2. In the meantime, heat the margarine in a large skillet. Add the onion and sauté over moderate heat until golden, about 5 minutes. Add the succotash and tomatoes; cook over moderate heat until well heated through, about 5 to 7 minutes.

3. When the noodles are done, drain and return them to the pot. Combine the noodles with the skillet mixture and the fresh parsley. Toss well, then season to taste with a bit of salt and lots of freshly ground pepper; toss again and serve.

Calories: 161	Total fat: 2 g	Protein: 5 g
Carbohydrate: 29 g	Cholesterol: 0 g	Sodium: 80 mg

DUTCH-STYLE SWEET-AND-SOUR SLAW

1-pound bag pre-grated coleslaw cabbage
1 small red bell pepper, cut into strips
⅓ cup honey or brown rice syrup
⅓ cup apple cider vinegar
2 tablespoons safflower or canola oil
½ teaspoon each of salt, celery or dill seed, and dry
  mustard

1. Combine the coleslaw cabbage and bell pepper strips in a large mixing bowl.

2. Combine the remaining ingredients in a small mixing bowl and whisk together. Pour over the slaw and toss well. Set aside to marinate, stirring once or twice before serving.

| Calories: 118 | Total fat: 4 g | Protein: 1 g |
| Carbohydrate: 19 g | Cholesterol: 0 g | Sodium: 192 mg |

Pantry staples
- ❏ Onion, 1 large
- ❏ Plum tomatoes, 28-ounce can (if not using fresh)
- ❏ Honey or brown rice syrup
- ❏ Apple cider vinegar
- ❏ Safflower or canola oil
- ❏ Celery or dill seed
- ❏ Dry mustard

Refrigerator staples
- ❏ Soy margarine

Shopping list: fresh foods and nonstaples
- ❏ Yolk-free ribbon egg noodles, 8- or 12-ounce package
- ❏ Frozen succotash (mixed corn and lima beans), 1-pound bag
- ❏ Fresh tomatoes, 1½ pounds
- ❏ Fresh parsley, 1 bunch
- ❏ Fresh string beans or zucchini, about 1 pound
- ❏ Fresh rye bread, 1 loaf
- ❏ Pre-grated coleslaw cabbage, 1-pound bag
- ❏ Red bell pepper, 1 small

_____ *MENU* _____

Angel Hair Pasta with Pine Nuts
and Sun-Dried Tomatoes

Italian Chopped Salad

Steamed broccoli

Broiled garlic toast

Serves 6

_____

Simple yet hearty, this meal tastes richer than it actually is. Teaming the Angel Hair Pasta with broiled garlic toast is gustatory paradise, as far as garlic lovers are concerned. The other accompaniments add a myriad of pleasing textures and flavors.

Strategy:

1. Follow the recipe for Angel Hair Pasta.

2. Preheat the broiler.

3. Prepare the Italian Chopped Salad.

4. Slice a loaf of Italian bread lengthwise. Spray each half with olive oil cooking spray. Broil the bread halves for 3 to 4 minutes, or until golden brown, watching carefully so as not to overbake them. Cover them with foil and keep in a closed, turned-off oven until needed.

5. Steam about a pound of precut broccoli florets until they're bright green.

ANGEL HAIR PASTA WITH PINE NUTS AND SUN-DRIED TOMATOES

10 to 12 ounces dried angel hair pasta (cappellini)
½ cup fresh parsley leaves (remove thick stems but don't be too fussy about small ones)
2 tablespoons olive oil, preferably extra-virgin
4 large garlic cloves, sliced
2 teaspoons dried basil or 2 tablespoons minced fresh basil, if available
¼ cup oil-cured sun-dried tomatoes, drained and thinly sliced
½ teaspoon dried red-pepper flakes (optional)
¼ cup grated Parmesan cheese or soy Parmesan
Salt and freshly ground pepper, to taste
¼ cup toasted pine nuts

1. Bring water for the pasta to a boil in a large pot.

2. Mince the parsley and set aside.

3. In the meantime, heat the oil in a heavy skillet over low heat and add the garlic. Sauté, stirring, until the garlic just begins to turn pale gold. Be careful not to let it burn or it will be bitter. Remove the pan from the heat; add the basil, dried tomatoes, and optional red-pepper flakes; toss to combine and set aside.

4. When the water comes to a full, rolling boil, add the pasta and cook until *al dente*. Drain the pasta, reserving the cooking liquid in a bowl set underneath the colander. Add 1 cup of the cooking liquid to the garlic mixture.

5. Place the pasta in a large serving bowl, and top with the garlic sauce and Parmesan cheese. Toss well, adding additional pasta cooking liquid if the mixture needs a bit more moisture. Season to taste with salt and pepper and toss again.

6. Top the pasta with the reserved parsley and toasted pine nuts. Pass around extra grated Parmesan or soy Parmesan when serving, if desired.

Calories: 174	Total fat: 9 g	Protein: 5 g
Carbohydrate: 17 g	Cholesterol: 3 g	Sodium: 72 mg

ITALIAN CHOPPED SALAD

It's not magic, just the brine green olives are packed in. The savory brine contains all the flavor and tang you'll need for this salad without adding salt or vinegar — try it and you'll see!

1 medium head Boston lettuce, thinly sliced
3 plum tomatoes, diced
½ cup small pitted black olives
½ cup small stuffed green olives
4 scallions, thinly sliced
½ medium cucumber, peeled and diced
2 tablespoons canola oil
3 to 4 tablespoons brine from green olives, to taste
Freshly ground black pepper, to taste

1. In a large salad bowl, combine the lettuce, tomatoes, black and green olives, scallions, and cucumber. Toss.

2. Just before serving, drizzle canola oil over the salad, then the green olive brine and toss well. Grind some fresh black pepper over the top and serve.

Calories: 77	Total fat: 7 g	Protein: 0 g
Carbohydrate: 4 g	Cholesterol: 0 g	Sodium: 208 mg

Strategy, continued

and tender-crisp to your liking. Drain and transfer the broccoli to a serving bowl.

6. Just before serving, rub the Italian bread with the open side of a peeled, halved clove of garlic.

Pantry staples
❏ Olive oil cooking spray
❏ Canola oil
❏ Light or extra-virgin olive oil
❏ Red-pepper flakes
❏ Dried basil
❏ Black olives, 1 can

Refrigerator staples
❏ Fresh garlic
❏ Green olives
❏ Grated Parmesan cheese or soy Parmesan

Shopping list: fresh foods and nonstaples
❏ Angel hair pasta (cappellini), 1-pound package
❏ Fresh precut broccoli florets, 1 pound
❏ Boston lettuce, 1 medium head
❏ Plum tomatoes, 3 medium
❏ Cucumber, 1 medium
❏ Scallions, 1 bunch
❏ Fresh parsley, 1 bunch
❏ Sun-dried tomatoes, oil-cured, 4 ounces
❏ Toasted pine nuts, about 2 ounces
❏ Italian bread, 1 long loaf

MENU

Peanut Butter Spirals

Cinnamon-Apple Glazed Baby Carrots

Sliced cucumbers, celery sticks, and tomatoes

Serves 6 to 8

Definitely a child-friendly menu, this features simple, familiar foods and flavors. Try this out on your most finicky eaters. Who knows, they may even ask for seconds!

Strategy:

1. Begin boiling water for the pasta.

2. Prepare the glazed carrots for cooking.

3. Begin cooking the pasta and the carrots. While they cook, prepare the peanut butter sauce.

4. Slice and arrange the raw vegetables.

5. Toss the hot, drained pasta with the peanut butter sauce.

PEANUT BUTTER SPIRALS

Kids love pasta and peanut butter, so this mild-flavored combination of the two should prove a hit. Adults might like to spice this up with hot chili oil or other hot sauce. This filling dish makes a generous portion, so you might serve it cold the next day for lunch.

10 ounces spiral or rotini pasta
½ cup peanut butter
¾ cup water or vegetable stock
3 tablespoons soy sauce
2 tablespoons white-wine vinegar or rice vinegar
1 tablespoon honey or rice syrup
½ teaspoon ground ginger
½ teaspoon chili powder
1½ cups frozen green peas, thawed
Chili oil or Tabasco sauce (optional)

1. Begin cooking the pasta.

2. Combine the remaining ingredients, except for the peas, in a blender or food processor fitted with a steel blade. Process until smooth.

3. When the pasta is just about done, toss the peas in to warm them, then drain and transfer them to a large serving bowl. Add the sauce and toss well.

Pass around chili oil or Tabasco sauce for anyone who'd like to spice up their dish.

Helpful tip: The peanut butter sauce thickens as it stands. Mix in more water if the dish sits for a while before serving, or before serving leftovers the next day.

Calories: 196	Total fat: 9 g	Protein: 8 g
Carbohydrate: 22 g	Cholesterol: 0 g	Sodium: 435 mg

CINNAMON-APPLE GLAZED BABY CARROTS

Using undiluted apple juice concentrate to cook the carrots adds a perfect touch of sweetness and moisture without the use of a refined sweetener or added fat.

1-pound bag fresh baby carrots
⅓ cup unsweetened apple juice concentrate, undiluted, thawed
½ teaspoon ground cinnamon

1. Combine all of the ingredients in a large saucepan and stir.

2. Bring to a simmer and cook over moderate heat for 15 to 20 minutes, covered, or until the carrots are tender-crisp.

3. Turn the heat up a bit, and cook the carrots uncovered 3 to 5 minutes more or until the liquid is reduced to a glaze.

Calories: 51	Total fat: 0 g	Protein: 0 g
Carbohydrate: 12 g	Cholesterol: 0 g	Sodium: 47 mg

Pantry staples
- ❑ Spiral pasta (rotelle or rotini)
- ❑ Peanut butter
- ❑ Soy sauce
- ❑ Honey or brown rice syrup
- ❑ White-wine vinegar or rice vinegar
- ❑ Ground ginger
- ❑ Chili powder
- ❑ Ground cinnamon
- ❑ Chili oil or Tabasco sauce

Freezer staples
- ❑ Frozen green peas
- ❑ Unsweetened apple juice concentrate

Shopping list: fresh foods and nonstaples
- ❑ Baby carrots, 1-pound bag
- ❑ Cucumbers
- ❑ Celery
- ❑ Tomatoes

MENU

Fettuccine in Green Chili Corn Sauce

Deviled Tomatoes

Fat-free tortilla chips

Carrot and jicama sticks

Serves 6

This is an offbeat marriage of Italian and Tex-Mex, but the combination of a picante sauce with mild pasta is sublime. The pasta dish is one that kids might really love without the chilies, so if little ones are part of the picture, omit the chilies from the recipe; instead place them in a bowl and pass around among the adults to top their pasta.

Strategy:

1. Begin cooking the pasta.

2. While the water comes to a boil, prepare the bread crumb mixture for Deviled Tomatoes and arrange it on the tomatoes.

3. Preheat the broiler.

4. Cook the fettuccine and continue with step 2 of the recipe.

5. Broil the tomatoes.

FETTUCCINE IN GREEN CHILI CORN SAUCE

Because this has a cold sauce, this pasta dish is good for warm weather.

½ pound fettuccine (spinach or regular, or half of each)
1-pound bag frozen corn kernels, thawed
2 cups (1 pound) low-fat cottage cheese
¼ cup fresh parsley or cilantro leaves
2 scallions, chopped
1 tablespoon extra-virgin olive oil
1 small red bell pepper, cut into thin strips
4-ounce can green chilies, mild or hot, as preferred
Salt and freshly ground pepper, to taste

1. Begin cooking the fettuccine. Just before draining, add the corn kernels to heat them.

2. In a food processor or blender, combine the cottage cheese, parsley or cilantro leaves, scallions, and olive oil. Process until smoothly pureed.

3. When the fettuccine-corn mixture is done, drain it well and combine it with the cottage cheese mixture, bell pepper, and green chilies in a large bowl. Season to taste with salt and pepper.

Calories: 257	Total fat: 3 g	Protein: 16 g
Carbohydrate: 40 g	Cholesterol: 65 g	Sodium: 510 mg

DEVILED TOMATOES

6 ripe plum tomatoes
2 slices whole-grain bread, torn into several pieces
2 teaspoons canola oil or soy margarine
2 to 3 pinches each of several dried herbs (try a combination of dried dill, basil, and summer savory)

1. Preheat the broiler in your oven or toaster oven.

2. Cut the tomatoes in half and arrange on a baking dish.

3. In a food processor fitted with a steel blade, combine the bread, oil or margarine, and dried herbs. Process to get even, coarse crumbs.

4. Sprinkle the crumbs over the tomatoes. Broil for 3 to 5 minutes, depending on the strength of your broiler, or until the crumbs are golden brown. Watch carefully so that they don't burn.

Calories: 61	Total fat: 2 g	Protein: 2 g
Carbohydrate: 8 g	Cholesterol: 0 g	Sodium: 70 mg

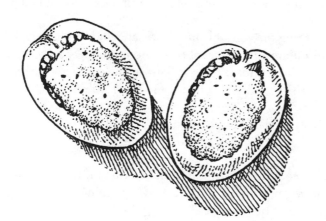

Strategy, continued

6. Finish the fettuccine recipe.

7. Cut the carrots and jicama into sticks at odd moments throughout the preparation of the meal.

Pantry staples
❏ Olive oil
❏ Green chilies, 4-ounce can, mild or hot
❏ Whole-grain bread, 2 sliced
❏ Canola oil
❏ Dried herbs (your choice)

Refrigerator staples
❏ Soy margarine (optional)

Freezer staples
❏ Frozen corn kernels, 1-pound bag

Shopping list: fresh foods and nonstaples
❏ Spinach fettuccine or regular fettuccine, or a combination
❏ Low-fat cottage cheese, 1-pound container
❏ Red bell pepper, 1 small
❏ Scallions, 1 bunch
❏ Plum tomatoes, 6
❏ Fresh parsley or cilantro
❏ Fresh carrots
❏ Fresh jicama (if unavailable, substitute white turnip)
❏ Tortilla chips, preferably fat-free

𝒨ENU

Vegetable Lo Mein

Gratin of Beets and Walnuts

Carrot and celery sticks

Serves 6

Lo Mein *is a term for noodle dishes enhanced with a variety of ingredients and then served in deep bowls with a fragrant broth. In this menu, a classic tofu-veggie stir-fry is made simple with the use of frozen stir-fry vegetables — a boon for those times when you have a yen for homemade Oriental but aren't in the mood for a lot of chopping!*

Strategy:

1. Preheat the oven. Assemble Gratin of Beets and Walnuts, place it in the oven, and set the timer for 15 minutes.

2. Mince the ginger and garlic; set aside. Assemble Vegetable Lo Mein through step 2; set aside.

3. Five minutes before the beets are ready, bring the Lo Mein ingredients to a simmer, add the pasta, and cook 3 to 4 minutes.

VEGETABLE LO MEIN

A one-dish Oriental superstar that's as good to look at as it is to eat. Use instant granules and water to make the broth (we like G. Washington or Romonoff brands, both available in supermarkets), or use canned vegetable broth. Fresh fettuccine, found in the refrigerator section in supermarkets, quickly cooks to a perfect texture in the flavorful broth.

½ pound extra-firm tofu
1 tablespoon dark sesame oil
6 cups vegetable broth (2 1-pound cans broth plus 2 cups water, or 3 packages instant granules mixed with 6 cups water)
1 tablespoon finely minced or grated fresh ginger
1 large clove garlic, finely minced
3 tablespoons bottled stir-fry or teriyaki sauce
1-pound package frozen mixed Oriental-style vegetables (unseasoned)
9- or 10-ounce package fresh fettuccine pasta
2 scallions, diagonally sliced

1. Cut the tofu into ½-inch-thick slices and blot between paper towels or a clean tea towel, then cut into ½-inch dice. Heat the sesame oil in a skillet and sauté the tofu in it over medium-high heat until golden on all sides, 4 to 5 minutes.

2. Bring the vegetable broth or water and broth granules to a simmer in a large soup pot. Add the ginger and garlic, and simmer for 2 minutes. Stir in the stir-fry sauce and vegetables, bring to a boil, and cook 1 minute.

3. Stir in the fettuccine and cook 4 minutes, or according to package directions, until *al dente*.

4. Gently stir the tofu into the mixture in the soup pot. Serve immediately in deep bowls, topping each serving with a scattering of scallions.

Calories: 272	Total fat: 11 g	Protein: 10 g
Carbohydrate: 33 g	Cholesterol: 74 g	Sodium: 599 mg

GRATIN OF BEETS AND WALNUTS

Happily, beets hold up extremely well through the canning process, and as in the case of beans, the hurried cook is encouraged to use them more often since they are so good in this form. Buying beets in cans saves about an hour's prep and cooking time.

2 1-pound cans sliced beets, drained (reserve liquid)
2 tablespoons undiluted orange juice concentrate, or more or less to taste
Vegetable oil cooking spray
½ small onion, finely chopped
¼ cup walnuts, coarsely chopped
Freshly ground pepper
3 tablespoons minced fresh parsley

1. Preheat the oven to 375 degrees.

2. Toss the beets with the orange juice concentrate and 2 tablespoons reserved beet liquid.

3. Spray an oblong, shallow baking dish with vegetable oil cooking spray and pile the beets in. Scatter the onion over the top, followed by the walnuts, then grind fresh pepper over all.

4. Cover tightly with a lid or foil and bake 15 minutes. Uncover, sprinkle with parsley, and serve.

Calories: 127	Total fat: 3 g	Protein: 3 g
Carbohydrate: 22 g	Cholesterol: 0 g	Sodium: 100 mg

Pantry staples
❏ Dark sesame oil
❏ Vegetable oil cooking spray
❏ Onions, small

Refrigerator staples
❏ Fresh garlic
❏ Carrots
❏ Celery

Freezer staples
❏ Orange juice concentrate

Shopping list: fresh foods and nonstaples
❏ Frozen Oriental vegetables (unseasoned), 1-pound bag
❏ Extra-firm tofu, ½ pound if bought by weight, or portion of a 1-pound tub
❏ Teriyaki or stir-fry sauce
❏ Canned sliced beets, 2 1-pound cans
❏ Fresh parsley, 1 bunch
❏ Fresh fettuccine pasta, 9- or 10-ounce package
❏ Scallions, 1 bunch
❏ Fresh ginger
❏ Walnuts, shelled
❏ Vegetable broth powder, 3 packages, or vegetable broth, 2 1-pound cans

MENU

Vermicelli with Fresh Tomato and Basil Sauce

Mozzarella slices with black olives

Corn-on-the-cob

Serves 6

This aromatic summer dish of pasta with an uncooked sauce will get you out of the kitchen quickly. Simple accompaniments make the whole meal a snap; it's light and satisfying at the same time.

Strategy:

1. Prepare the corn and begin cooking it in a large pot of boiling water. Or microwave it if you prefer, allowing the appropriate time per ear of corn according to the wattage of your unit.

2. Prepare the pasta recipe.

3. Slice the mozzarella cheese and arrange it attractively on a platter. Scatter small, brine-cured olives or sliced black olives over the slices. If desired, drizzle with a bit of extra-virgin olive oil.

VERMICELLI WITH FRESH TOMATO AND BASIL SAUCE

Nothing other than the very ripe, flavorful tomatoes of summer will do for this dish.

10 to 12 ounces vermicelli (extra-thin spaghetti)
2½ pounds ripe, juicy tomatoes, cored and quartered
3 tablespoons olive oil, preferably extra-virgin
¼ to ½ cup fresh basil leaves, to taste
¼ cup parsley leaves
1 to 2 scallions, coarsely chopped
Juice of ½ lemon
Salt and freshly ground pepper, to taste
Grated Parmesan cheese or soy Parmesan (optional)

1. Cook the pasta until *al dente*. When it's done, drain and transfer it to a large serving bowl.

2. In the meantime, prepare the tomatoes, then combine them in a food processor with the oil, basil, parsley, scallions, and lemon juice. Pulse on and off until all are finely chopped, with some texture remaining — don't puree!

3. Toss the cooked pasta with the tomato sauce, then season to taste with salt and freshly ground pepper. Pass around grated Parmesan cheese or soy Parmesan, if desired.

Calories: 177	Total fat: 7 g	Protein: 4 g
Carbohydrate: 24 g	Cholesterol: 0 g	Sodium: 17 mg

Pantry staples
- ❏ Vermicelli (extra-thin spaghetti), 12-ounce or 1-pound box
- ❏ Extra-virgin olive oil
- ❏ Pitted black olives, portion of 1-pound can (if not using brine-cured olives)

Refrigerator staples
- ❏ Lemon, 1
- ❏ Grated Parmesan cheese or soy Parmesan (optional)

Shopping list: fresh foods and nonstaples
- ❏ 2½ pounds ripe, juicy tomatoes
- ❏ Fresh basil, 1 small bunch
- ❏ Fresh parsley, 1 small bunch
- ❏ Scallions, 1 bunch
- ❏ Corn-on-the-cob, 6 ears, or as needed
- ❏ Mozzarella cheese, fresh or part-skim, 8 ounces
- ❏ Brine-cured olives, about ¼ pound

_____ *MENU* _____

Rotini with Spinach, Chickpeas,
and Sun-Dried Tomatoes

Carrot and Raisin Salad

Fresh bread of your choice

Serves 4 to 6

_____

*There's a real stick-to-your-ribs quality to
this pasta dish, and the slight sweetness of
the classic carrot and raisin salad is a perfect counterpoint to its strong, savory flavors.*

_____

Strategy:

1. Begin cooking the pasta; thaw spin-
    ach in microwave if necessary.

2. Continue the pasta recipe from step
    3 through step 4.

3. Prepare the Carrot and Raisin Salad.

4. Complete the pasta recipe.

ROTINI WITH SPINACH, CHICKPEAS, AND SUN-DRIED TOMATOES

½ pound rotini (spiral pasta)
2 tablespoons extra-virgin olive oil
2 to 3 cloves garlic, minced
1 small green bell pepper, cut into strips
10-ounce package frozen chopped spinach,
    thawed and squeezed
14-ounce can Italian plum tomatoes, chopped,
    with liquid
1-pound can chickpeas, drained and rinsed
¼ cup chopped oil-cured sun-dried tomatoes
1 teaspoon dried oregano
Salt and freshly ground pepper, to taste
¼ to ½ teaspoon dried hot red-pepper flakes
    (optional)
Grated Parmesan cheese or soy Parmesan for topping
    (optional)

1. Begin cooking the pasta.

2. Heat the oil in a large skillet. Add the garlic and bell
pepper and sauté over moderate heat until the garlic is
lightly golden and the bell pepper is slightly wilted, about
3 to 4 minutes.

3. Add the spinach, plum tomatoes, chickpeas, sun-dried
tomatoes, and oregano to the skillet. Stir together and
simmer gently for 8 to 10 minutes.

5. When the pasta is done, drain it and transfer it to a
large serving container. Toss with the skillet mixture. Season to taste with salt and pepper, and add the red-pepper
flakes, if desired. Toss again, and serve, passing around
grated Parmesan cheese or soy Parmesan, if desired.

_____

Calories: 268	Total fat: 7 g	Protein: 9 g
Carbohydrate: 39 g	Cholesterol: 0 g	Sodium: 70 mg

CARROT AND RAISIN SALAD

A food processor is a must for preparing this salad quickly.

½ pound carrots, peeled
1 cup raisins
1 tablespoon lemon juice
3 tablespoons light brown sugar
½ teaspoon ground cinnamon
1 tablespoon poppy seeds

1. Grate the carrots in a food processor, using the coarse grating attachment.

2. Transfer the carrots to a serving bowl, add the remaining ingredients, and mix together thoroughly.

Calories: 127	Total fat: 0 g	Protein: 1 g
Carbohydrate: 30 g	Cholesterol: 0 g	Sodium: 26 mg

Pantry staples
❑ Rotini (spiral) pasta, 1-pound box
❑ Extra-virgin olive oil
❑ Italian plum tomatoes, 14-ounce can
❑ Chickpeas, 1-pound can
❑ Dried oregano
❑ Dried red-pepper flakes (optional)
❑ Raisins
❑ Light brown sugar
❑ Ground cinnamon

Refrigerator staples
❑ Fresh garlic
❑ Grated Parmesan cheese or soy Parmesan (optional)

Freezer staples
❑ 10-ounce package frozen chopped spinach

Shopping list: fresh foods and nonstaples
❑ Green bell pepper
❑ Carrots
❑ Sun-dried tomatoes, oil-cured, about 2 ounces
❑ Lemon, 1
❑ Poppy seeds
❑ Fresh bread

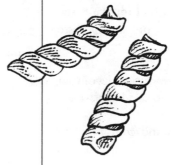

ＭＥＮＵ

Fettuccine with Pesto Florentine

Italian Herbed Bread

Tossed green salad

Serves 6

The flavors of garlic and greens combined with nuts and cheese create the rich taste of pesto in a lightened version. This can be made off-season, too, as it requires only a small amount of basil in tandem with convenient frozen chopped spinach. The term Florentine, *by the way, is applied to Italian dishes that contain spinach.*

Strategy:

1. Preheat the oven to 350 degrees, then prepare the Italian Herbed Bread and place it in the oven to crisp. Set the timer for 10 minutes and check if it's done; if not, set for an additional 5 minutes. When the bread is done, remove it from the oven and wrap it in foil until needed.

2. Bring water to a boil for the pasta, and while it cooks, prepare the Pesto Florentine sauce.

3. Prepare greens and vegetables of your choice for a tossed salad; set aside.

4. Drain the pasta and combine with the pesto sauce. Dress the salad as desired.

FETTUCCINE WITH PESTO FLORENTINE

12-ounce box dry fettuccine pasta, regular or spinach
2 10-ounce packages frozen chopped spinach, thawed (see Note)
⅓ cup walnuts or toasted pine nuts
2 large or 3 medium cloves garlic
½ cup fresh basil, leaves and stems
¼ cup extra-virgin olive oil
Juice of 1 large lemon
Salt and freshly ground pepper, to taste
¼ cup grated Parmesan cheese or soy Parmesan

1. Bring water for the pasta to a boil in a large pot. Set the oven temperature to 150 degrees, and place a large serving bowl in it to warm while preparing the sauce.

2. Squeeze as much liquid out of the thawed spinach as possible; set aside.

3. Add the pasta to the boiling water and cook according to package directions until *al dente*. Drain in a colander, then place the pasta-filled colander in the large pot, cover, and set aside.

4. Place the nuts and garlic in a blender or in a food processor fitted with a steel blade and process until finely chopped. Add the spinach and basil. With the machine running, pour in the oil in a thin stream. Pour in the lemon juice, salt, and pepper. Process until well blended. Add the Parmesan and pulse on and off just until mixed.

5. Place the pasta in the warm bowl, add the sauce, and mix thoroughly. Serve immediately.

Note: If you prefer, by all means substitute fresh spinach. You'll need 2 10- or 12-ounce bags of fresh spinach; buy the "triple-washed" type to make its use easier, but take into account the extra time it takes to stem, steam, and chop it.

| Calories: 334 | Total fat: 15 g | Protein: 12 g |
| Carbohydrate: 38 g | Cholesterol: 97 g | Sodium: 176 mg |

ITALIAN HERBED BREAD

1 loaf Italian bread, preferably whole-grain
Olive oil cooking spray
½ teaspoon salt
Several grinds of black pepper (about ¼ teaspoon)
2 teaspoons dried Italian herb mix
2 tablespoons minced fresh parsley

1. Preheat the oven to 350 degrees. Cut 1-inch-thick slices almost but not quite all the way through to the bottom crust of the bread. Place the loaf on a baking sheet. Gently spread the slices apart and spray both sides of each one with olive oil spray.

2. In a small bowl, combine the remaining ingredients. Spread the slices again, and sprinkle the mixture between them. Bake 10 to 15 minutes, or until the bread is hot and crisp.

| Calories: 162 | Total fat: 5 g | Protein: 6 g |
| Carbohydrate: 24 g | Cholesterol: 0 g | Sodium: 399 mg |

Pantry staples
❑ Extra-virgin olive oil
❑ Olive-oil cooking spray
❑ Dried Italian herb mix

Refrigerator staples
❑ Grated Parmesan cheese or soy Parmesan
❑ Lemon, 1 large
❑ Fresh garlic

Freezer staples
❑ Frozen chopped spinach, 2 10-ounce packages

Shopping list: fresh foods and nonstaples
❑ Fresh basil, 1 bunch
❑ Fresh parsley, 1 small bunch
❑ Walnuts, shelled
❑ Fettuccine, regular or spinach, 12-ounce package
❑ Salad vegetables of your choice
❑ Fresh Italian bread, 1 loaf, preferably whole-grain

_____ *MENU* _____

Simple Sesame-Soy Oriental
Noodles

Broccoli, Carrot, and Cashew
Stir-Fry with Tofu

Serves 4

What? You're going to order Chinese take-out again? Put down that phone! Add this simple, colorful meal to your repertoire, and you'll think twice before dialing. What's even better, it might actually get to your table quicker than a meal that you have to order and wait for — plus, this is lower in fat than Chinese takeout.

Strategy:

1. Begin cooking the noodles.

2. While the water comes to a boil, begin working on the broccoli and carrot stir-fry dish through step 2, then cook the noodles.

3. Prepare the sauce for the noodle dish.

4. Continue and finish the vegetable stir-fry, then continue and finish the noodle dish. Garnish each and serve.

SIMPLE SESAME-SOY ORIENTAL NOODLES

½ pound udon or soba noodles (see Note)
1½ tablespoons canola oil
2 teaspoons dark sesame oil
2 to 3 tablespoons soy sauce, or more or less to taste
1 tablespoon honey or rice syrup
1 teaspoon grated fresh ginger, or ¼ teaspoon ground ginger
1 teaspoon rice vinegar or white-wine vinegar
2 to 3 scallions, sliced

1. Begin cooking the noodles.

2. Whisk the remaining ingredients, except the scallions, together in a bowl.

3. When the noodles are done, drain and transfer them to a large serving container. Drizzle the sauce over them, then quickly toss together.

4. Scatter the sliced scallions over the top.

Note: Soba (also known as buckwheat noodles) and udon are delicious whole-grain noodles that are readily available in natural food stores. If you're in a pinch, use regular spaghetti or linguine; the results will be good, though not quite as interesting.

Calories: 166	Total fat: 8 g	Protein: 4 g
Carbohydrate: 20 g	Cholesterol: 0 g	Sodium: 632 mg

BROCCOLI, CARROT, AND CASHEW STIR-FRY WITH TOFU

1 pound firm tofu
1 tablespoon canola oil
2 tablespoons soy sauce
3 to 4 tablespoons dry white wine or sherry
5 heaping cups precut broccoli florets
3 large carrots, peeled and cut diagonally
⅓ cup unsalted toasted cashews, chopped
Extra soy sauce

1. Cut the tofu ½ inch thick crosswise, blot the slices between paper towels, then cut into ½-inch dice.

2. Heat the oil and 2 tablespoons of soy sauce in a wok or large skillet. Add the tofu dice, turn the heat up to moderately high, and stir-fry for 2 to 3 minutes.

3. Add the wine or sherry, broccoli, and carrots to the wok or skillet. Cover and steam for 5 minutes over moderate heat.

4. Uncover the wok or skillet and turn the heat up to moderately high once again. Stir-fry for 2 to 3 minutes more, or until most of the liquid has been absorbed.

5. Top the stir-fry with the chopped cashews and serve from the wok or skillet. Pass around extra soy sauce when serving for anyone who might want it.

Calories: 245	Total fat: 13 g	Protein: 12 g
Carbohydrate: 16 g	Cholesterol: 0 g	Sodium: 569 mg

Pantry staples
❑ Dark sesame oil
❑ Soy sauce
❑ Honey or rice syrup
❑ Rice vinegar or white-wine vinegar
❑ Dry white wine or sherry
❑ Canola or safflower oil
❑ Ground ginger (if not using fresh)

Refrigerator staples
❑ Carrots

Shopping list: fresh foods and nonstaples
❑ Udon or soba (buckwheat) noodles, ½-pound package
❑ Firm tofu, 1 pound
❑ Precut broccoli florets, about 1 pound
❑ Scallions, 1 bunch
❑ Fresh ginger
❑ Toasted unsalted cashews

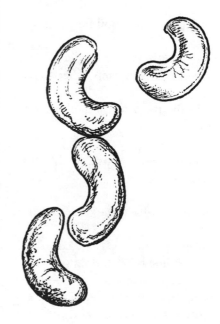

MENU

Pasta Puttanesca

Gorgonzola-Lettuce Wedges

Warm kaiser rolls

Serves 6

Puttanesca is a dish whose robust and satisfying combination of flavors had its start in the night life of the red light districts of Naples where "working girls" created it and then went on to make it famous. We leave it to you to imagine sultry Neapolitan nights and bowls of this savory pasta, teamed with a salad spiked with another famous Italian, Gorgonzola cheese.

Strategy:

1. Bring water to a boil for the pasta.

2. Prepare the Gorgonzola-Lettuce Wedges through step 1. Set aside.

3. Add the pasta to the boiling water and cook.

4. Continue with steps 2 and 3 of the pasta recipe.

5. Place the rolls in the oven to warm.

6. When the pasta is done, arrange it in a serving bowl and do step 4.

7. Continue with step 2 for the Gorgonzola-Lettuce Wedges.

PASTA PUTTANESCA

10 to 12 ounces linguine
¼ cup dry red wine
1 tablespoon light or extra-virgin olive oil
1 medium shallot, minced
2 large garlic cloves, minced
14-ounce can Italian plum tomatoes, lightly drained and chopped
14-ounce can crushed or pureed tomatoes
½ cup pitted black olives, coarsely chopped
½ cup stuffed green olives, coarsely chopped
½ teaspoon dried oregano
Freshly ground pepper, to taste
½ cup chopped fresh parsley
Grated Parmesan cheese or soy Parmesan for topping (optional)

1. Bring water to a boil in a large pot and cook the pasta until *al dente*.

2. In the meantime, combine the wine, olive oil, shallot, and garlic in a heavy, medium-sized skillet. Bring the mixture to a boil, cover, and cook 2 minutes. Alternatively, combine the mixture in a microwavable dish and microwave on High for 30 seconds to 1 minute, depending on the wattage of your unit.

3. Add tomatoes, black and green olives, and oregano. Cover and simmer 12 minutes, or microwave on High for 3 to 4 minutes.

4. When the linguine is done, drain and transfer it to a large serving bowl and top it with the olive sauce and freshly ground pepper. Toss, then sprinkle with parsley. If desired, top with a sprinkling of Parmesan cheese.

Calories: 162	Total fat: 6 g	Protein: 3 g
Carbohydrate: 22 g	Cholesterol: 0 g	Sodium: 319 mg

GORGONZOLA-LETTUCE WEDGES

Anything more than a crisp wedge of lettuce, creamy Gorgonzola, and a splash of lemon juice would be gilding the lily.

1 head Boston or Bibb lettuce
Fresh lemon juice (from ½ to 1 lemon, to taste)
4 ounces Gorgonzola cheese, crumbled (see Variation)

1. Cut lettuce in 6 wedges, making sure to leave each wedge attached to the core in order to hold its shape. Take a thin slice off the base of the core so the wedge will sit upright on the plate.

2. Squeeze fresh lemon over each wedge sparingly. Sprinkle each with a tablespoon or two of crumbled cheese.

Variation: If Gorgonzola cheese is unavailable, substitute blue cheese.

Calories: 79	Total fat: 5 g	Protein: 4 g
Carbohydrate: 2 g	Cholesterol: 14 g	Sodium: 269 mg

Pantry staples
- ❏ Linguine, 1-pound package
- ❏ Light or extra-virgin olive oil
- ❏ Dry red wine
- ❏ Italian plum tomatoes, 14-ounce can
- ❏ Crushed or pureed tomatoes, 14-ounce can
- ❏ Pitted black olives, 8-ounce can, or portion of 1-pound can
- ❏ Dried oregano

Refrigerator staples
- ❏ Grated Parmesan cheese
- ❏ Lemon, 1
- ❏ Fresh garlic
- ❏ Pimiento-stuffed green olives

Shopping list: fresh foods and nonstaples
- ❏ Boston or Bibb lettuce, 1 large head
- ❏ Gorgonzola cheese (substitute blue cheese if unavailable), 4 ounces
- ❏ Shallot, 1 large
- ❏ Parsley, 1 bunch
- ❏ Fresh kaiser rolls

MENU

Pasta with Garlic and Oil

Baked Breaded Zucchini,
Mushrooms, and Tofu

Cherry tomatoes and sliced bell
peppers

Serves 4 to 6

---

*This simple, fragrant pasta dish is a classic,
called* aglia olio, *meaning garlic and oil,
in Italian. Complemented by savory baked
vegetables and tofu, it's a meal of pleasing
and familiar flavors.*

Strategy:

1. Prepare the recipe for the baked vegetables with tofu.

2. While it is baking, prepare the pasta recipe.

3. While the pasta cooks, wash some cherry tomatoes and slice a red or green bell pepper or two.

4. Assemble the pasta dish.

PASTA WITH GARLIC AND OIL

10 to 12 ounces extra-thin spaghetti (vermicelli) or
   angel hair (cappellini)
¼ cup extra-virgin olive oil, divided
4 to 6 cloves garlic, minced
¼ cup grated Parmesan cheese or soy Parmesan
¼ cup finely chopped fresh parsley
Salt and freshly ground pepper, to taste

1. Bring water to a boil and cook the pasta at a steady simmer until *al dente*.

2. Meanwhile, heat half of the oil in a small skillet. Sauté the garlic over medium-low heat until golden, but do not allow to brown. Set aside until needed.

3. When the pasta is done, drain (reserve some of the cooking water, caught in a bowl under the colander) and transfer it to a large serving bowl. Add the sautéed garlic, the remaining oil, and the remaining ingredients. Toss well. If the mixture needs a bit more moisture, drizzle in some of the cooking water. Season to taste with salt and pepper, toss again, and serve.

| Calories: 210 | Total fat: 11 g | Protein: 5 g |
| Carbohydrate: 20 g | Cholesterol: 3 g | Sodium: 77 mg |

BAKED BREADED ZUCCHINI, MUSHROOMS, AND TOFU

Breading
½ cup toasted wheat germ
1 teaspoon salt-free herb-and-spice seasoning mix
1 teaspoon Italian herb seasoning mix
½ teaspoon salt

1 medium zucchini
1 pound extra-firm tofu
8 ounces medium-sized white mushrooms
Vegetable or olive oil cooking spray
Marinara sauce or canned pureed tomatoes, warmed

1. Preheat the oven to 450 degrees.

2. Combine the breading ingredients in a large mixing bowl and stir together.

3. Cut the zucchini lengthwise into quarters, then into eighths, then cut the pieces into 2-inch or so lengths.

4. Cut the tofu into ½-inch-thick slices and blot briefly on paper towels or clean tea towels to remove excess moisture. Then cut into ½-inch-thick "fingers" about 1½ to 2 inches long.

5. Combine the mushrooms, zucchini, and tofu with the breading mixture and toss gently until the vegetables and tofu are coated.

6. Line a large baking sheet with foil. Spray lightly with cooking oil spray, then place the breaded vegetables and tofu on the baking sheet in a single layer. Spray briefly and evenly over the top with cooking spray, then bake for 12 to 15 minutes, or until the zucchini and mushrooms are just tender and the crumbs begin to crisp.

7. Pass around some warmed marinara sauce or tomato puree for anyone that wants to spoon some over their serving.

Calories: 136	Total fat: 5 g	Protein: 11 g
Carbohydrate: 11 g	Cholesterol: 0 g	Sodium: 225 mg

Pantry staples
❏ Extra-virgin olive oil
❏ Vegetable or olive oil cooking spray
❏ Salt-free herb-and-spice seasoning mix
❏ Italian herb seasoning blend
❏ Marinara sauce, 1-pound jar, or crushed or pureed tomatoes, 14-ounce can

Refrigerator staples
❏ Fresh garlic
❏ Grated Parmesan cheese or soy Parmesan
❏ Toasted wheat germ

Shopping list: fresh foods and nonstaples
❏ Extra-thin spaghetti (vermicelli), or angel hair pasta (cappellini), 12-ounce or 1-pound box
❏ Tofu, extra-firm, 1 pound
❏ Zucchini, 1 medium
❏ Mushrooms, medium-sized, 8 ounces
❏ Fresh parsley, 1 bunch
❏ Cherry tomatoes, 1 pint
❏ Green or red bell pepper, 1 or 2 medium

⎯⎯⎯ MENU ⎯⎯⎯

Pasta Mexicana

Hot corn bread or corn muffins
(purchased)

Tossed greens with cucumbers,
broccoli florets, and olives

Serves 6

⎯⎯⎯⎯⎯⎯⎯⎯⎯⎯⎯

Pasta becomes a one-dish meal when enveloped in a hefty sauce of beans, tomato sauce, corn, and bell peppers. You'll leave the table feeling quite full, and yet the dish is amazingly low in fat. Do mind the type of corn bread or muffins you buy though — this type of pastry can come laden with fat and sugar. If good fresh corn bread or muffins aren't available to you, substitute fresh, warmed wheat tortillas.

⎯⎯⎯⎯⎯⎯⎯⎯⎯⎯⎯

Strategy:

1. Prepare the recipe for Pasta Mexicana.

2. Warm the corn bread or corn muffins in a 300-degree oven or toaster oven.

3. While the sauce is simmering and the pasta is cooking, prepare a simple tossed salad of lettuce, raw or lightly steamed broccoli florets, sliced cucumbers, and pitted black olives. If available, add a few chunks of diced ripe avocado. A low-fat buttermilk or ranch dressing works well with this meal.

PASTA MEXICANA

8 to 10 ounces spiral pasta (rotelle or rotini)
1½ tablespoons light or extra-virgin olive oil
1 large onion, halved and thinly sliced
1 to 2 cloves garlic, minced
1 medium green bell pepper, cut into thin strips
1 medium red bell pepper, cut into thin strips
28-ounce can crushed or pureed tomatoes
1-pound can pinto or red beans, drained and rinsed
1 cup thawed frozen corn kernels
1 teaspoon chili powder
1 teaspoon ground cumin
1 teaspoon dried oregano
Salt, to taste
Pre-grated reduced-fat cheddar cheese or grated
    cheddar-style soy cheese for topping (optional)

1. Bring water to a boil in a large pot and cook the pasta at a steady simmer until *al dente*.

2. Meanwhile, heat the oil in a deep, heavy saucepan. Add the onion and garlic and sauté over medium heat, covered, until limp, about 4 minutes. Stir once or twice during that time. Layer the bell pepper strips over the onion and cover. Sauté for another 3 minutes or so without stirring, then stir and sauté, uncovered, for another 2 minutes.

3. Add the remaining ingredients except the grated cheese and bring to a simmer, then simmer gently while the pasta cooks.

4. When the pasta is done, drain it well and combine in a large serving container with the sauce. Toss well to combine. If desired, pass around a bowl of grated cheese so that everyone can top their serving with a small amount.

Calories: 267	Total fat: 5 g	Protein: 9 g
Carbohydrate: 48 g	Cholesterol: 0 g	Sodium: 53 mg

Pantry staples
- ❏ Spiral pasta (rotelle or rotini), 1-pound box
- ❏ Light or extra-virgin olive oil
- ❏ Onion, 1 large
- ❏ Crushed tomatoes, 28-ounce can
- ❏ Pinto or red beans, 1-pound can
- ❏ Black pitted olives, portion of 8-ounce or 1-pound can
- ❏ Chili powder
- ❏ Ground cumin
- ❏ Dried oregano

Refrigerator staples
- ❏ Fresh garlic

Freezer staples
- ❏ Corn kernels, portion of 10-ounce box or 1-pound bag

Shopping list: fresh foods and nonstaples
- ❏ Green bell pepper, 1 medium
- ❏ Red bell pepper, 1 medium
- ❏ Salad ingredients recommended (lettuce, cucumbers, fresh broccoli, avocado), or as desired
- ❏ Reduced-fat buttermilk or ranch dressing
- ❏ Reduced-fat pre-grated cheddar cheese or cheddar-style soy cheese (optional)
- ❏ Fresh corn bread or corn muffins

───── *MENU* ─────

Curried Pasta with Ricotta, Red Onion, Peas, and Raisins

Tossed salad

Chapatis or other flatbread

Serves 6 to 8

───────────────

This creamy, mildly curried pasta dish makes for a super-easy one-dish meal. My young kids love this — it's sort of a fancy version of macaroni and cheese, after all, and I think they like the sweet surprise of the raisins. All that's needed to complete this meal is a brightly colored tossed salad and some chewy flatbread. Look for Indian-style chapatis in a natural food store; otherwise you may substitute pitas or mini-pitas from the supermarket, or any other interesting flatbread you may come upon.
— N. A.

Strategy:

1. Do steps 1 through 3 of the pasta recipe.

2. While the pasta cooks and the onions sauté, prepare a tossed salad. Make it colorful with shredded red cabbage, carrots, sliced tomatoes, dark green lettuce leaves, red bell peppers, and other salad vegetables of your choice. Dress as desired.

CURRIED PASTA WITH RICOTTA, RED ONION, PEAS, AND RAISINS

12 ounces spiral pasta or ziti
1½ tablespoons canola oil
1 large red onion, chopped
15-ounce container part-skim ricotta cheese
½ cup low-fat milk
10-ounce package (2 cups) frozen green peas
⅔ cup dark raisins
1 to 2 teaspoons good-quality curry powder, to taste
1 teaspoon salt, or to taste

1. Bring water to a boil in a large cooking pot. Cook the pasta at a steady simmer.

2. Meanwhile, heat the oil in a medium-sized skillet. Add the onion and sauté, covered, until it is limp and just beginning to turn golden, about 7 to 8 minutes.

3. While the pasta cooks and the onion sautés, combine the ricotta and milk in a large serving bowl. Stir well until smooth.

4. Just before the pasta is done, add the green peas to the pot and cook until the pasta is *al dente* and the peas are thoroughly warmed. Drain well and add to the ricotta mixture in the bowl, stirring well to coat the pasta.

5. Stir in the raisins, then season to taste with curry powder and salt.

Calories: 253	Total fat: 7 g	Protein: 12 g
Carbohydrate: 33 g	Cholesterol: 19 g	Sodium: 91 mg

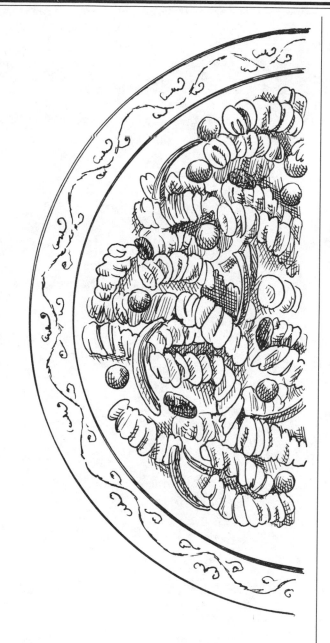

Strategy, continued

3. Warm the chapatis or other flatbread, if desired.

4. Complete the pasta recipe.

Pantry staples
❑ Spiral pasta or ziti, 1-pound box
❑ Canola oil
❑ Dark raisins
❑ Curry powder

Refrigerator staples
❑ Low-fat milk

Freezer staples
❑ Green peas, 10-ounce box, or portion of 1-pound bag

Shopping list: fresh foods and nonstaples
❑ Red onion, 1 large
❑ Ricotta cheese, part-skim, 15-ounce container
❑ Salad ingredients of your choice (if following the suggestion, you'll need red cabbage, dark green lettuce, carrots, tomatoes, and red bell peppers, plus whatever other vegetables you'd like to use)
❑ Fresh chapatis, pita bread or mini-pitas, or other flatbread of your choice

Chapter Two

MOSTLY MEXICAN

The earthy and simple home-cooking style presented in this chapter is an amalgam of Southwestern, Tex-Mex, and basic Mexican ideas. In all of the aforementioned cuisines, there are a few key ingredients, with a wonderful range of variations. What's best about these ingredients — wheat and corn tortillas, beans, rice, corn, and of course, green chilies — is that they're all easily available, and all come in convenient, ready-to-use versions right on the supermarket shelf.

Here we present basic, vegetarian versions of some well-loved classics, plus a handful of offbeat composites. These simple, hearty menus, full of the lively flavor combinations that have made this style of food so popular, are likely to win a permanent place in your repertoire — even on those days when you're not necessarily in a great hurry to get supper on the table!

Black Bean Tostadas
Green Beans with Tomatoes
Microwaved potatoes (optional)

Rice and Bean Enchiladas
Chunky Guacamole
Sautéed zucchini or summer squash
Fat-free tortilla chips

Seitan Fajitas
Southwestern Corn Slaw

Basic Bean Burritos
Golden Rice

Mexican Lasagna (Tortilla Casserole)
Mixed Squash Sauté
Simple salad of curly lettuce, cherry tomatoes, and bell peppers

Tofu Migas (Scrambled Tofu with Tortillas)
Corn-Olive Salad
Steamed Broccoli

Southwestern Zucchini-Corn Chowder
Chili-Cheese Tortilla Roll-Ups
Fresh fruit plate

Quick Spanish Rice
Nachos with Chili con Queso
Simple coleslaw

Bulgur Tacos
Frijoles Borrachos (Beer-Stewed Pinto Beans)
Sliced avocado

Quick Black Bean Soup
Mexican Pizza
Simple tossed salad

MENU

Black Bean Tostadas

Green Beans with Tomatoes

Microwaved potatoes (optional)

Serves 6

Neatness is not a virtue of a tostada dinner. Rather, tostadas are to be enjoyed as a sensuous (and slightly messy) adventure, so in addition to the side dishes recommended here, be sure to provide plenty of napkins — and enjoy!

Strategy:

1. If you're serving potatoes, scrub 6 medium potatoes and microwave on High for the recommended time per potato according to the wattage of your unit. You need to use at least a 750-watt unit for all 6 potatoes to be done within the allotted time for this menu.

2. Prepare the tostada recipe through step 4.

3. While the tortillas are baking, prepare the green bean recipe.

4. Prepare the toppings for the tostadas and let everyone assemble their own.

BLACK BEAN TOSTADAS

A tostada is a crisp tortilla piled generously with any variety of toppings, often including beans, crisp lettuce, and fresh tomatoes and chilies, or salsa. To eat one, either pick up the whole thing and take bites, or break it into smaller pieces to pick up and eat.

1 tablespoon olive oil
1 medium onion, chopped
2 cloves garlic, minced
2 1-pound cans black beans, drained and rinsed
Juice of ½ lemon
1 teaspoon ground cumin
12 good-quality corn tortillas (see Note)

Toppings
Shredded lettuce, as needed
Low-fat yogurt, low-fat sour cream, or soy yogurt
Chunky salsa, mild to hot, as preferred

1. Preheat the oven to 375 degrees.

2. Heat the oil in a deep, heavy saucepan. Add the onion and garlic and sauté until the onion is lightly golden, about 5 minutes.

3. Add the remaining ingredients, except the tortillas, plus ¼ cup water and bring to a simmer. With a potato masher, mash some of the beans so that the liquid becomes thick and saucy.

4. Spread the tortillas on a baking sheet and place it in the center of the preheated oven. Bake for 10 minutes, or until crisp and dry. Remove them from the oven and place them on a serving platter.

5. Place the shredded lettuce, yogurt or sour cream, and bottled salsa in separate serving bowls and let everyone assemble their tostadas as follows: a layer each of the black bean mixture; the yogurt or sour cream; and the lettuce, topped with some salsa.

Note: For successful tostadas, the corn tortillas must be of a good quality and fresh. Don't use those that have been sitting in your freezer for weeks or months; rather than bake to a crisp texture, they will taste hard and stale.

The following analysis does not include the toppings:

Calories: 361	Total fat: 5 g	Protein: 16 g
Carbohydrate: 63 g	Cholesterol: 0 g	Sodium: 545 mg

GREEN BEANS WITH TOMATOES

This simple side dish is wonderful with the tender green beans of summer. Just be aware that trimming and steaming a pound of fresh green beans will add at least 10 minutes to the preparation time of this menu.

1-pound bag green beans, whole or cut
1 pound ripe tomatoes, diced
1 tablespoon extra-virgin olive oil
1 tablespoon red-wine vinegar or apple cider vinegar
Salt and freshly ground pepper, to taste

1. Place the trimmed green beans in a large skillet with about an inch of water. Steam, covered, for 5 to 7 minutes over moderate heat, or until bright green and tender-crisp. Drain, then return to the skillet.

2. Stir in the tomatoes, cover, and cook another 2 to 3 minutes, just until the tomatoes have lost their raw quality. Transfer the green bean–tomato mixture to a serving bowl, toss in the oil and vinegar, and season to taste with salt and pepper.

Calories: 59	Total fat: 2 g	Protein: 1 g
Carbohydrate: 8 g	Cholesterol: 0 g	Sodium: 10 mg

Pantry staples
- ❏ Extra-virgin olive oil
- ❏ Onion, 1 medium
- ❏ Black beans, 2 1-pound cans
- ❏ Ground cumin
- ❏ Red-wine vinegar or apple cider vinegar

Refrigerator staples
- ❏ Fresh garlic
- ❏ Lemon, 1

Shopping list: fresh foods and nonstaples
- ❏ Dark green lettuce
- ❏ Good-quality corn tortillas, 1 dozen (normally we list these as a freezer staple, but it's best to buy them just before you need them for this recipe)
- ❏ Low-fat yogurt, low-fat sour cream, or soy yogurt
- ❏ Bottled salsa, chunky style, mild to hot as preferred
- ❏ Green beans, frozen, 1-pound bag (or use fresh if preferred)
- ❏ Tomatoes, ripe, 1 pound
- ❏ Potatoes (optional), 6 or more

___MENU___

Rice and Bean Enchiladas

Chunky Guacamole

Sautéed zucchini or summer squash

Fat-free tortilla chips

Serves 4

Putting rice into rather than alongside an enchilada might seem offbeat, but it's really not unusual. The combination of rice and beans makes for a pleasing textural effect. This is Mexican-style fast food at its best!

Strategy:

1. Preheat the oven to 425 degrees.

2. Cook the rice. While it's cooking, prepare the remaining ingredients for the filling, then combine and finish the recipe.

3. Quarter two medium zucchini lengthwise and cut them into approximately 2-inch spears. Sauté them in a little olive oil. If desired, and if time allows, sprinkle the zucchini with a tablespoon or so of finely chopped parsley before serving.

4. Put the enchiladas in the oven; set the timer for 10 minutes.

RICE AND BEAN ENCHILADAS

2-serving portion quick-cooking brown rice
2 1-pound cans pinto or pink beans, drained and rinsed
2 scallions, finely chopped
1 teaspoon ground cumin
1 teaspoon dried oregano
8 good-quality corn tortillas, at room temperature
1 cup pre-grated Monterey Jack cheese or grated cheddar-style soy cheese
Bottled chunky salsa or tomatillo salsa (salsa verde)

1. Preheat the oven to 425 degrees.

2. Following package directions, cook a 2-serving portion of quick brown rice in a large saucepan. When it's done, stir in the beans, scallions, and seasonings.

3. The tortillas should be soft and pliable; if necessary, wrap them in foil and place them in the hot oven for a minute or two.

4. Divide the filling among the tortillas, spreading it down the center of each, and roll them up. Arrange the tortillas, opening side down, in a lightly oiled baking dish. They should fit snugly so that they remain shut while baking.

5. Sprinkle the tortillas evenly with the cheese and bake 10 minutes. Arrange two enchiladas on each plate per serving and pass around the salsa for topping.

Calories: 454	Total fat: 9 g	Protein: 18 g
Carbohydrate: 76 g	Cholesterol: 19 g	Sodium: 714 mg

CHUNKY GUACAMOLE

2 medium ripe (but not overripe) avocados
1 cup diced fresh tomato
½ medium red bell pepper, finely diced
2 tablespoons chopped fresh parsley or cilantro
Juice of ½ lemon
½ teaspoon ground cumin
Salt and freshly ground pepper, to taste

1. Peel and pit the avocados, place them in a serving bowl, and mash coarsely, leaving the texture chunky.

2. Add the remaining ingredients and mix well. Cover until serving time.

Calories: 186	Total fat: 12 g	Protein: 2 g
Carbohydrate: 16 g	Cholesterol: 0 g	Sodium: 13 mg

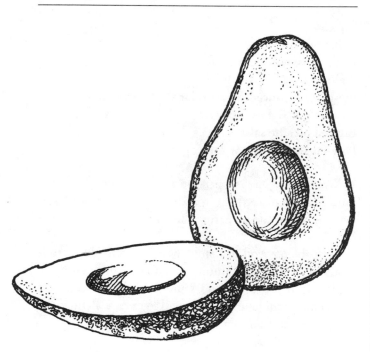

Strategy, continued

5. Prepare the guacamole. Put it into a serving container, then place it on a plate surrounded by tortilla chips.

Pantry staples
- ❏ Quick-cooking brown rice
- ❏ Pinto or pink beans, 2 1-pound cans
- ❏ Ground cumin
- ❏ Dried oregano
- ❏ Olive oil, light (for sautéing squash)

Refrigerator staples
- ❏ Lemon, 1

Freezer staples
- ❏ Corn tortillas, 8

Shopping list: fresh foods and nonstaples
- ❏ Chunky-style salsa or tomatillo salsa (salsa verde)
- ❏ Pre-grated Monterey Jack cheese or cheddar-style soy cheese, 8 ounces
- ❏ Avocados, 2 medium
- ❏ Tomatoes, about 2 medium
- ❏ Red bell pepper, 1 medium
- ❏ Scallions, 1 bunch
- ❏ Parsley or cilantro, 1 bunch
- ❏ Zucchini or yellow summer squash, 2 medium
- ❏ Tortilla chips, preferably fat-free

MENU

Seitan Fajitas

Southwestern Corn Slaw

Serves 6

With just the right amount of spiciness and a gustatory grip that just won't let go until the last scrap is gone, this is a fajita that really satisfies. It will pass muster with the fussiest of fajita fans and will be a pleasant surprise to anyone who hasn't yet tried seitan. Best of all, it all comes together in less than 25 minutes.

Strategy:

1. Prepare the slaw and set aside.

2. Wrap the fajita wrappers or wheat tortillas in foil and place in oven or toaster oven to warm at 250 degrees.

3. Prepare the fajita filling and arrange garnishes as directed. Place fajita wrappers or wheat tortillas on a platter and let everyone assemble their own fajitas.

SEITAN FAJITAS

Seitan, or cooked wheat gluten, is a delicious, high-protein product that's useful as an analog of beef chunks but without the cholesterol and with virtually no fat. You can make your own from a mix that's available in natural food stores (it takes only minutes to prepare, but needs some time to simmer), or you can buy seitan ready-made.

12 whole wheat fajita wrappers or wheat tortillas
1 tablespoon olive oil
1 small onion, chopped
2 cloves garlic, minced
1 red bell pepper, sliced in strips
1 green bell pepper, sliced in strips
1 pound fresh seitan, thinly shredded
1 tablespoon chili powder, or to taste
2 tablespoons soy sauce

Garnishes
1 ripe but firm avocado
1 to 2 teaspoons lemon juice
2 plum tomatoes, finely diced
Pre-grated reduced-fat cheddar cheese or grated
    cheddar-style soy cheese
Bottled picante salsa
Low-fat sour cream or soy yogurt

1. Wrap the fajita wrappers or wheat tortillas in aluminum foil and place them in a 250-degree oven or toaster oven to heat while preparing the filling.

2. Heat the olive oil in a small heavy skillet, add the onion, and sauté a few minutes to soften slightly. Add the garlic and bell peppers and sauté 5 minutes more. Add the seitan shreds, chili powder, and soy sauce. Reduce the heat to low and simmer 5 minutes more.

3. Mash the avocado with a little lemon juice. Place it in a small bowl, then put the diced tomato, shredded cheese, picante sauce, and sour cream or soy yogurt into separate, small serving bowls.

4. Let everyone assemble their own fajitas as follows: a scoop of filling down the center, topped with a small amount of each of the garnishes. Roll up and eat at once!

The following analysis is based on 2 fajitas per serving:

Calories: 317	Total fat: 6 g	Protein: 30 g
Carbohydrate: 35 g	Cholesterol: 0 g	Sodium: 556 mg

SOUTHWESTERN CORN SLAW

Now that cabbage is available already washed, cored, and shredded, slaw is the answer to every busy cook's dream. Just add other veggies and good-quality corn, and it's a done deal.

8-ounce package pre-shredded coleslaw cabbage
10-ounce package frozen corn kernels, thawed
1 small red onion, thinly sliced
4 scallions, white and green parts, thinly sliced
1 small zucchini, diced
1 red bell pepper, seeded and chopped
¼ cup chopped parsley, or to taste

Dressing
¼ cup apple cider vinegar
2 tablespoons light olive oil
1 teaspoon Dijon mustard
1 teaspoon honey or brown rice syrup
1 teaspoon ground cumin

1. In a large bowl, combine all the salad ingredients.

2. In a small bowl, combine the dressing ingredients and whisk together. Pour over the salad, toss well, cover, and let stand until needed.

Calories: 108	Total fat: 4 g	Protein: 2 g
Carbohydrate: 15 g	Cholesterol: 0 g	Sodium: 36 mg

Pantry staples
❏ Apple cider vinegar
❏ Dijon mustard
❏ Honey or brown rice syrup
❏ Light olive oil
❏ Chili powder
❏ Ground cumin
❏ Soy sauce
❏ Onion, 1 small

Refrigerator staples
❏ Lemon, 1
❏ Fresh garlic

Freezer staples
❏ Frozen corn kernels, 10-ounce package, or portion of 1-pound bag

Shopping list: fresh foods and nonstaples
❏ Whole wheat fajita wrappers or wheat tortillas, 1 dozen
❏ Fresh seitan, 1 pound
❏ Pre-shredded coleslaw cabbage, 8-ounce package, or portion of 1-pound package
❏ Zucchini, 1 small
❏ Red bell peppers, 2
❏ Green bell pepper, 1
❏ Avocado, 1 ripe, firm
❏ Plum tomatoes, 2 medium
❏ Red onion, 1 small
❏ Scallions, 1 bunch
❏ Parsley, 1 small bunch
❏ Pre-grated reduced-fat cheddar cheese or cheddar-style soy cheese, 8 ounces
❏ Picante salsa
❏ Low-fat sour cream or soy yogurt

ℳℰℕ𝒰

Basic Bean Burritos

Golden Rice

Serves 6

These super-quick burritos are so much a part of my quick-cooking repertoire that I took them for granted and almost forgot to include them in this collection. It took a request from a friend, who wondered if she could look forward to an easy burrito menu as part of this book, to remind me to pass this along. After all, simple is often best!
—N. A.

Strategy:

1.   Prepare the Golden Rice.

2.   Prepare the burritos.

BASIC BEAN BURRITOS

12 6-inch flour tortillas
1 tablespoon light or extra-virgin olive oil
2 cloves garlic, minced
2 1-pound cans pinto beans, drained and rinsed
1 teaspoon ground cumin
Bottled picante sauce
Pre-grated reduced-fat cheddar cheese or grated
    cheddar-style soy cheese

Garnishes
Shredded lettuce
Black olives
Tomato wedges

1. Wrap the tortillas in foil and place them in a 300-degree oven or toaster oven to warm.

2. Heat the oil in a large, heavy saucepan. Add the garlic and sauté over moderate heat for 2 minutes.

3. Add the pinto beans, cumin, and ½ cup water. Bring to a simmer, then mash the beans with a potato masher until all have been broken and the mixture is thick and chunky. Stir the beans, cook another minute, then remove from the heat.

4. Assemble the burritos as follows, allowing two per serving: Spoon some bean filling down the center of the tortilla, followed by a bit of picante sauce, then a light sprinkling of cheese. Roll up the tortillas and place seam side down on the individual plates.

5. Garnish each serving with lettuce, olives, and tomato wedges. These burritos may simply be picked up and eaten.

| Calories: 347 | Total fat: 8 g | Protein: 13 g |
| Carbohydrate: 55 g | Cholesterol: 15 g | Sodium: 749 mg |

GOLDEN RICE

6-serving portion quick-cooking brown rice
2 scallions, chopped
1 teaspoon chili powder
½ teaspoon turmeric
2 teaspoons extra-virgin olive oil
Salt, to taste

1. Cook the rice according to package directions. When the water comes to a boil, stir in the rice, followed by the remaining ingredients. When the rice is done, fluff it with a fork.

Calories: 129	Total fat: 1 g	Protein: 3 g
Carbohydrate: 25 g	Cholesterol: 0 g	Sodium: 0 mg

Pantry staples
❑ Light or extra-virgin olive oil
❑ Pinto beans, 2 1-pound cans
❑ Ground cumin
❑ Quick-cooking brown rice
❑ Chili powder
❑ Turmeric
❑ Black olives, 8-ounce or
   1-pound can

Refrigerator staples
❑ Fresh garlic

Freezer staples
❑ Wheat tortillas, 1 dozen

*Shopping list: fresh foods and
   nonstaples*
❑ Pre-grated reduced-fat cheddar
   cheese or cheddar-style soy cheese
❑ Picante sauce, 1 bottle
❑ Lettuce, 1 small head, any variety
❑ Tomatoes, 4 medium or 6 plum

MENU

Mexican Lasagna
(Tortilla Casserole)

Mixed Squash Sauté

Simple salad of curly lettuce, cherry
tomatoes, and bell peppers

Serves 6

---

*There's nothing terribly complicated about
rolling up a few enchiladas, but for those
times when even that seems like too much
to do, this casserole is perfect. It gives you
all the familiar and lively flavors of the
Southwest, with absolutely no fuss. All you
need to do is mix, layer, and bake — few
casseroles this hearty can be made in such
short order.*

Strategy:

1. Preheat the oven to 400 degrees. Prepare the tortilla casserole and place
   it in the oven. Set the timer for 12
   minutes.

2. Prepare the squash sauté.

3. While the squash sautés, make a
   simple salad of curly lettuce, cherry
   tomatoes, and bell peppers, drizzled
   with a few drops of olive oil and red-
   wine vinegar.

MEXICAN LASAGNA
(Tortilla Casserole)

1-pound can pinto, pink, or black beans,
 drained and rinsed
14-ounce can diced or stewed tomatoes
4-ounce can chopped mild green chilies
2 cups frozen corn kernels, thawed
2 scallions, minced
½ teaspoon ground cumin
½ teaspoon dried oregano
8 corn tortillas
1½ cups pre-grated Monterey Jack cheese or
 grated cheddar-style soy cheese
Reduced-fat sour cream or soy yogurt for topping
 (optional)

1. Preheat the oven to 400 degrees.

2. Combine the first 7 ingredients in a mixing bowl. Mix
thoroughly.

3. Lightly oil a wide, 2-quart casserole dish and layer as
follows: 4 tortillas, overlapping one another; half of the
bean mixture; half of the cheese. Repeat the layers.

4. Bake the casserole for 12 to 15 minutes, or until the
cheese is bubbly. Let stand for a minute or two, then cut
into squares to serve. Top each serving, if desired, with a
small scoop of sour cream or soy yogurt.

Helpful tip: Kids who have gotten to the stage when they
like beans are likely to enjoy this casserole, so you may
want to make it minus the chilies to suit their preference
for milder flavors. Pass a bowl of chopped chilies around
for those who wish to top their serving with them.

Calories: 336	Total fat: 10 g	Protein: 16 g
Carbohydrate: 45 g	Cholesterol: 25 g	Sodium: 166 mg

MIXED SQUASH SAUTÉ

This recipe calls for zucchini and yellow summer squashes, which are available year-round, but any tender squash, such as pattypan, may be substituted or added.

1½ tablespoons extra-virgin olive oil
1 small onion, finely chopped
1 medium zucchini, sliced
2 medium yellow summer squashes, sliced
¼ cup black olives, sliced
Salt and freshly ground pepper, to taste

1. Heat the oil in a large skillet. Sauté the onion until it is translucent.

2. Add 2 tablespoons of water to the skillet, followed by the zucchini and yellow squashes, and stir. Cover and "sweat" the squashes until they are just tender, about 5 minutes. Stir once in the interim.

3. Stir in the black olives and season with salt and pepper.

Calories: 65	Total fat: 4 g	Protein: 1 g
Carbohydrate: 5 g	Cholesterol: 0 g	Sodium: 45 mg

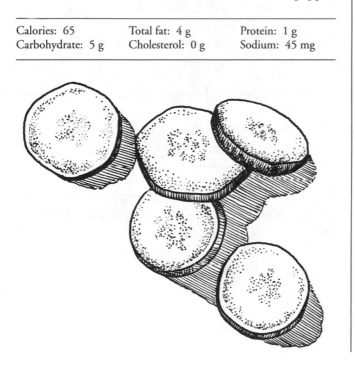

Pantry staples
❑ Pinto, pink, or black beans, 1-pound can
❑ Crushed tomatoes, 14-ounce can
❑ Ground cumin
❑ Dried oregano
❑ Olive oil, extra-virgin
❑ Onion, 1 small
❑ Green chilies, chopped mild, 4-ounce can
❑ Black olives, portion of 8-ounce or 1-pound can
❑ Red-wine vinegar (for salad)

Refrigerator staples
❑ Reduced-fat sour cream or soy yogurt (optional)

Freezer staples
❑ Frozen corn kernels, 10-ounce package, or portion of a 1-pound bag
❑ Corn tortillas, 8

Shopping list: fresh foods and nonstaples
❑ Pre-grated Monterey Jack cheese, 8-ounce package, or 8 ounces cheddar-style soy cheese
❑ Zucchini, 1 medium
❑ Yellow summer squashes, 2 medium
❑ Scallions, 1 bunch
❑ Curly lettuce, 1 medium head
❑ Cherry tomatoes, 1 pint
❑ Red bell pepper, 1 medium
❑ Green bell pepper, 1 medium

MENU

Tofu Migas
(Scrambled Tofu with Tortillas)

Corn-Olive Salad

Steamed broccoli

Serves 6

Some years ago, when my husband and I traveled throughout the Southwest, we enjoyed chili-infused breakfasts such as migas, *a popular dish of scrambled eggs with tortilla bits. Now I make* migas *with tofu, which to my mind makes the dish heartier and more befitting a place at the dinner table.*

— N. A.

Strategy:

1. Prepare the Tofu Migas.

2. While it simmers, prepare the Corn-Olive Salad.

3. Steam about 1 pound of precut broccoli florets in a steamer basket (or in a large saucepan with about 1 inch of water) until bright green and tender-crisp.

TOFU MIGAS
(Scrambled Tofu with Tortillas)

Migas *means "crumbs" in Spanish, which in this classic dish refers to the small pieces of corn tortilla. This is a great way to use up less-than-perfectly-fresh tortillas, the purpose for which this dish (traditionally made with eggs and not tofu) was invented. The mélange of lively flavors makes this a great dish for tofu skeptics.*

1 tablespoon light olive oil
1 medium onion, finely chopped
1 pound firm tofu, drained
6 corn tortillas, torn or cut into approximately
    1-inch pieces
3 plum tomatoes, diced
14-ounce can crushed or pureed tomatoes
4-ounce can chopped green chilies, mild to hot,
    as preferred
1 teaspoon ground cumin
Salt, to taste
¾ cup reduced-fat pre-grated cheddar cheese or grated
    cheddar-style soy cheese (optional)
Bottled chunky-style salsa or tomatillo salsa (optional)

1. Heat the oil in a large skillet. Sauté the onion over moderate heat until lightly golden, about 4 to 5 minutes.

2. Cut the tofu into ½-inch-thick slices, and blot the slices gently between paper towels or a clean tea towel. Then cut them into ½-inch dice.

3. Add the tofu to the skillet, followed by all the remaining ingredients except the cheese and salsa, and stir together gently. Cover and cook over moderate heat for 10 minutes.

4. If using the grated cheese or soy cheese, sprinkle it over the top, cover, and cook another 3 to 4 minutes, or until the cheese is melted. If desired, pass around salsa for topping each serving.

Calories: 203	Total fat: 7 g	Protein· 9 g
Carbohydrate: 26 g	Cholesterol: 0 g	Sodium: 46 mg

CORN-OLIVE SALAD

Corn salads are easy, savory, and relishlike, and so compatible with Southwestern flavors.

Dressing
1 tablespoon olive oil
3 tablespoons apple cider vinegar
2 teaspoons honey or rice syrup
1 tablespoon minced fresh dill, or ½ teaspoon
    dried dill

1-pound package frozen corn kernels,
    thoroughly thawed
1 medium green bell pepper, cut into 1-inch strips
¼ cup black olives, coarsely chopped
¼ cup green olives, coarsely chopped
1 celery stalk, diced
1 scallion, finely chopped
Freshly ground pepper, to taste

1. Combine the dressing ingredients in a small bowl and whisk together.

2. Combine the remaining ingredients in a serving bowl. Pour the dressing over them, then toss quickly. Season to taste with freshly ground pepper.

Calories: 111	Total fat: 4 g	Protein: 2 g
Carbohydrate: 17 g	Cholesterol: 0 g	Sodium: 156 mg

Pantry staples
❑ Light olive oil
❑ Onion, 1 medium
❑ Crushed or pureed tomatoes,
    14-ounce can
❑ Chopped green chilies, mild or hot,
    4-ounce can
❑ Ground cumin
❑ Apple cider vinegar
❑ Honey or rice syrup
❑ Dried dill (if not using fresh)
❑ Black olives, portion of 8-ounce or
    1-pound can

Refrigerator staples
❑ Green olives, pitted
❑ Celery, 1 stalk

Freezer staples
❑ Corn kernels, 1-pound bag
❑ Corn tortillas, 6

*Shopping list: fresh foods and
    nonstaples*
❑ Plum tomatoes, 3
❑ Firm tofu, 1 pound
❑ Pre-grated reduced-fat cheddar
    cheese, 8-ounce package, or
    cheddar-style soy cheese (optional)
❑ Chunky-style salsa or tomatillo
    salsa (salsa verde), 1 bottle
    (optional)
❑ Fresh precut broccoli florets, about
    1 pound
❑ Green bell pepper, 1 medium
❑ Scallions, 1 bunch
❑ Fresh dill, 1 small bunch

MENU

Southwestern Zucchini-Corn Chowder

Chili-Cheese Tortilla Roll-Ups

Fresh fruit plate

Serves 6

A savory quick soup teamed with a practically effortless tortilla concoction and a plate of refreshing fruits makes for an offbeat yet satisfying meal. Try this when you're in the mood for something a little unusual.

Strategy:

1. Make the soup.

2. While it simmers, preheat the oven to 400 degrees, then prepare the Chili-Cheese Tortilla Roll-Ups through step 3.

3. Prepare a fruit plate of fresh seasonal fruits. This meal is nicely finished with cantaloupe or honeydew sections, unpeeled grapefruits sliced into eighths, and seedless grapes. Or, serve a variety of melons: watermelon, cantaloupe, and honeydew.

4. Five minutes before needed, put the tortillas for the roll-ups into the oven. Set the timer for 5 minutes, bake, then remove from the oven,

SOUTHWESTERN ZUCCHINI-CORN CHOWDER

1½ tablespoons light olive oil
1 large onion, finely chopped
2 cloves garlic, minced
1 medium red bell pepper, diced
1 cup diced fresh tomatoes, or the equivalent of drained, canned plum tomatoes
2 medium zucchini, cut into ½-inch dice
2 tablespoons unbleached flour
10-ounce package (2 cups) frozen corn kernels
3 cups water or canned vegetable stock
½ teaspoon ground cumin
1 teaspoon salt-free herb-and-spice blend
1 cup low-fat milk or soy milk
Salt and freshly ground pepper, to taste

1. Heat the oil in a soup pot. Sauté the onion, garlic, and bell pepper over moderate heat, covered, until all are tender, about 5 minutes.

2. While the onion-garlic mixture is sautéing, prepare the tomatoes and zucchini. Sprinkle the flour into the onion-garlic mixture and stir until blended.

3. Add the remaining ingredients to the pot except the last two. Bring to a simmer over moderately high heat, then lower the heat and cook at a gentle but steady simmer for 10 minutes.

4. Stir in the milk or soy milk, then season to taste with salt and pepper.

Calories: 167	Total fat: 5 g	Protein: 5 g
Carbohydrate: 27 g	Cholesterol: 2 g	Sodium: 46 mg

CHILI-CHEESE TORTILLA ROLL-UPS

12 6-inch flour tortillas
8-ounce package grated reduced-fat cheddar cheese, or
    8 ounces cheddar-style soy cheese, grated
4-ounce can chopped green chilies, mild to hot, as
    preferred

1. Preheat the oven to 400 degrees.

2. Arrange the tortillas flat in a single layer on two baking sheets that are either lightly oiled or sprayed with vegetable oil spray.

3. Sprinkle the cheese evenly over their entire surface, then, with a teaspoon, place a thin stripe of green chilies down the center of each.

4. Bake for 5 minutes, or just until the cheese is melted. Remove each tortilla to a serving plate with a wide spatula, then roll up. Allow two per serving, and serve with the soup.

The following analysis is based on 2 roll-ups per serving:

Calories: 360	Total fat: 14 g	Protein: 14 g
Carbohydrate: 30 g	Cholesterol: 40 g	Sodium: 556 mg

Strategy, continued,

and roll up as directed. Serve the roll-ups with the soup, then finish the meal with the fruit.

Pantry staples
❏ Light olive oil
❏ Onion, 1 large
❏ Canned vegetable stock (optional)
❏ Chopped green chilies, 4-ounce can, mild to hot, as preferred
❏ Ground cumin
❏ Salt-free herb-and-spice blend
❏ Unbleached white flour

Refrigerator staples
❏ Low-fat milk or soy milk
❏ Fresh garlic

Freezer staples
❏ Frozen corn kernels, 10-ounce package, or portion of 1-pound bag
❏ Wheat tortillas, 1 dozen

Shopping list: fresh foods and nonstaples
❏ Red bell pepper, 1 medium
❏ Ripe tomatoes, about 2 medium (out of season, replace with 14-ounce can plum tomatoes, drained)
❏ Zucchini, 2 medium
❏ Pre-grated reduced-fat cheddar cheese, 8-ounce package, or 8 ounces cheddar-style soy cheese
❏ Fresh fruit of your choice, in season: any combination of melons, watermelon, grapefruit, grapes

_____ MENU _____

Quick Spanish Rice

Nachos with Chili con Queso

Simple coleslaw

Serves 6 to 8

There's something fun and festive about nachos — tortilla chips with a chili-infused cheese sauce. But you need not save this for a festive occasion; go ahead and make it for an everyday meal and add a little fun to an ordinary day!

Strategy:

1. Combine a 1-pound bag of pre-shredded coleslaw cabbage with a dressing of your choice: bottled Italian, ranch, or coleslaw dressing (preferably in reduced-fat versions), reduced-fat mayonnaise, or better yet, commercially prepared tofu mayonnaise. Toss well and set aside. At the end, if time allows, you might embellish the slaw with sliced bell peppers.

2. Prepare and cook the Quick Spanish Rice.

3. Prepare the Chili con Queso.

QUICK SPANISH RICE

6-serving portion quick-cooking brown rice
8-ounce can (1 cup) tomato sauce
2 scallions, finely chopped
1 teaspoon chili powder
½ teaspoon ground cumin
½ teaspoon dried oregano
1 cup frozen green peas, thawed
Salt and freshly ground pepper, to taste

1. In a deep, heavy saucepan, cook the rice according to package directions, replacing 1 cup of the water recommended with 1 cup of tomato sauce. Stir in the scallions and seasonings and bring to a simmer. Cover and cook according to package directions, about 5 minutes.

2. Stir in the peas, then season to taste with salt and pepper. Keep covered until needed.

Calories: 159	Total fat: 0 g	Protein: 4 g
Carbohydrate: 34 g	Cholesterol: 0 g	Sodium: 213 mg

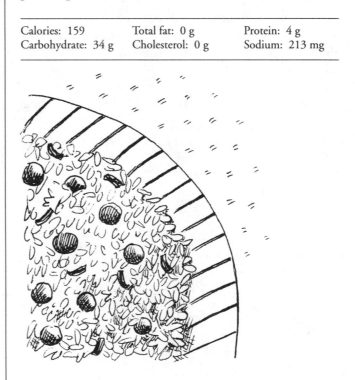

NACHOS WITH CHILE CON QUESO

2½ tablespoons unbleached flour
1 cup low-fat milk
1 medium tomato, finely diced
2 cups pre-grated Monterey Jack or reduced-fat
    cheddar cheese
4-ounce can chopped mild green chilies
¼ cup sliced black olives (optional)
8-ounce bag good-quality tortilla chips, preferably fat-
    free

1. Combine the flour with ¼ cup water in a small bowl or
a cup and stir together until dissolved. Set aside.

2. Heat the milk in a large saucepan. Just before it comes
to a simmer, slowly whisk in the dissolved flour mixture.
Stir in the diced tomatoes.

3. Stir the grated cheese in, one-half cup at a time. Let
each batch of cheese melt before stirring in the next.

4. Stir in the green chilies and the black olives, if desired,
and remove from the heat.

5. Spread the tortilla chips on a large platter. With a ladle,
drizzle the sauce over them. Serve with a wide spatula to
each individual plate.

Calories: 263	Total fat: 12 g	Protein: 13 g
Carbohydrate: 25 g	Cholesterol: 30 g	Sodium: 216 mg

Pantry staples
❏ Quick-cooking brown rice
❏ Tomato sauce, 8-ounce can
❏ Chili powder
❏ Ground cumin
❏ Dried oregano
❏ Chopped green chilies, 4-ounce
    can, mild to hot, as preferred
❏ Unbleached flour
❏ Black olives, portion of 8-ounce or
    1-pound can (optional)

Refrigerator staples
❏ Low-fat milk

Freezer staples
❏ Frozen green peas, portion of
    10-ounce package or 1-pound bag

*Shopping list: fresh foods and
    nonstaples*
❏ Pre-shredded coleslaw cabbage,
    1-pound bag
❏ Pre-grated Monterey Jack or
    reduced-fat cheddar cheese,
    8-ounce package
❏ Tomato, 1 medium
❏ Good-quality tortilla chips,
    preferably fat-free, 8- to
    10-ounce bag
❏ Scallions, 1 bunch

̶̶̶̶̶̶ 𝓜𝓔𝓝𝓤 ̶̶̶̶̶̶

Bulgur Tacos

**Frijoles Borrachos
(Beer-Stewed Pinto Beans)**

Sliced avocado

Serves 6

Bulgur, which is presteamed, cracked wheat, makes an outstanding substitute for the traditional ground beef filling in tacos, and is readily available in natural food stores and many supermarkets. These tacos are so flavorful that we've done away with the requisite shredded cheese, resulting in a low-fat treat. Complemented by pinto beans and avocado, this is a great meal for hearty appetites.

Strategy:

1. Begin cooking the bulgur as directed in step 1 of the Bulgur Tacos recipe. Continue through step 2 of the recipe.

2. While the onion-pepper mixture for the above sautés, prepare and cook the Frijoles Borrachos. Remove from the heat when done; serve directly from the saucepan if desired.

3. Prepare the shredded lettuce, diced tomatoes, and sliced olives for tacos. Place each in individual serving bowls.

BULGUR TACOS

¾ cup raw bulgur
1 tablespoon olive oil
1 medium onion, finely chopped
1 small red or green bell pepper, finely diced
2 cloves garlic, minced
½ cup thick tomato sauce or canned tomato puree
2 teaspoons chili powder
12 taco shells

Garnishes
**Shredded lettuce, about 3 loosely packed cups
2 medium tomatoes, diced
½ cup sliced black olives
Bottled salsa or picante sauce, mild to hot, as desired,
     or bottled tomatillo sauce (salsa verde)**

1. Combine the bulgur with 1½ cups of water in a small saucepan. Bring to a boil, then cover and cook at a steady simmer for 15 minutes, or until the water is absorbed.

2. In the meantime, heat the oil in a medium-sized skillet. Sauté the onion over moderate heat for 2 to 3 minutes, or until translucent. Add the diced bell pepper and garlic and sauté until all are golden, about another 5 minutes.

3. When the bulgur is done, transfer it to the skillet and add the tomato sauce and chili powder. Cook, stirring, until the mixture is well blended, then remove from the heat and cover.

4. Place the taco shells on a platter. Prepare the garnishes and place each in separate bowls.

5. Just before serving, transfer the bulgur mixture to a covered serving container. Have everyone assemble their own tacos as follows: Line each taco shell with a handful of shredded lettuce, followed by a scoop of the bulgur mixture. Garnish the top with diced tomatoes, black olives, and salsa or picante sauce.

The following analysis includes garnishes:

Calories: 255	Total fat: 9 g	Protein: 4 g
Carbohydrate: 40 g	Cholesterol: 0 g	Sodium: 525 mg

FRIJOLES BORRACHOS
(Beer-Stewed Pinto Beans)

This is a simplified version of a classic Southwestern recipe. The beer lends a mellow flavor and enticing aroma.

2 1-pound cans pinto beans, drained and rinsed
½ cup light beer
3 to 4 scallions, sliced
2 to 3 tablespoons chopped mild green chilies (about half of a 4-ounce can), to taste
1 teaspoon ground cumin

1. Combine all the ingredients in a large saucepan and bring to a simmer.

2. With a potato masher, mash about half of the beans. Simmer gently but steadily for another 2 to 3 minutes, or until the liquid base becomes a thick sauce.

Helpful tips: This dish thickens up as it stands. If you're not using it immediately, or if you're reheating leftovers, add a small amount of water to loosen the consistency.

If you happen to have some fresh cilantro, adding a handful of chopped leaves to this dish at the end of its cooking time lends a special flair to the flavor.

Calories: 164	Total fat: 0 g	Protein: 8 g
Carbohydrate: 30 g	Cholesterol: 0 g	Sodium: 233 mg

Strategy, continued

4. Slice two ripe, firm avocados and arrange on a small plate.

5. Transfer the bulgur mixture to a small, lidded casserole dish, and arrange the taco shells on a platter. Have everyone assemble their own tacos as directed in the recipe.

Pantry staples
❏ Olive oil
❏ Onion, 1 medium
❏ Tomato sauce or tomato puree
❏ Black olives
❏ Pinto beans, 2 1-pound cans
❏ Chopped mild green chilies, 4-ounce can
❏ Chili powder
❏ Ground cumin

Refrigerator staples
❏ Fresh garlic

Shopping list: fresh foods and nonstaples
❏ Bulgur, small box, or about ½ pound if bought in bulk
❏ Avocados, 2 medium
❏ Bell pepper, green or red, 1 small
❏ Lettuce, any variety, 1 head
❏ Tomatoes, 2 medium
❏ Salsa or picante sauce, mild to hot, as desired
❏ Scallions, 1 bunch
❏ Taco shells, 1 dozen
❏ Beer, preferably a light variety

⸺ MENU ⸺

Quick Black Bean Soup

Mexican Pizza

Simple tossed salad

Serves 6 to 8

Here's a great meal to make when you're expecting last-minute company and don't have even an hour to spend in the kitchen. Fast and festive, the colors and flavors presented here are crowd pleasers.

Strategy:

1. Prepare the soup.

2. Preheat the oven to 400 degrees, then prepare the Mexican Pizza.

3. While the pizzas are baking and cooling, prepare a very simple tossed salad. You might like to try a combination of dark green lettuce leaves, broccoli florets, sliced cucumbers, and toasted sunflower or pumpkin seeds, dressed with just a touch of extra-virgin olive oil and lemon juice.

QUICK BLACK BEAN SOUP

Making a soul-satisfying soup in such short order is a rarity, but canned black beans are so flavorful that they do the trick perfectly.

1 tablespoon extra-virgin olive oil
1 large onion, finely chopped
3 to 4 cloves garlic, finely chopped
4 1-pound cans black beans, drained and rinsed
Juice of ½ lemon
½ teaspoon ground cumin
½ teaspoon dried oregano
2 tablespoons finely chopped fresh parsley
Freshly ground pepper, to taste

Toppings
Reduced-fat sour cream, low-fat yogurt, or soy yogurt
3 to 4 scallions, thinly sliced

1. Heat the oil in a large soup pot. Sauté the onion over moderate heat until translucent, about 3 to 4 minutes. Add the garlic and sauté until the onion is lightly golden, another 3 to 4 minutes.

2. Add the remaining ingredients, except the toppings, along with 4 cups of water, and bring to a simmer.

3. Mash some of the beans with a potato masher, just enough to thicken the liquid base of the soup. Cover and simmer gently but steadily for 10 minutes.

4. Top each serving with a scoop of sour cream, yogurt, or soy yogurt, and a sprinkling of sliced scallion.

Helpful tip: If you have leftovers of this soup, it will thicken up. Either dilute it with a bit of extra water, or leave it thick and serve over hot cooked brown rice as a delicious sauce.

Calories: 221	Total fat: 2 g	Protein: 11 g
Carbohydrate: 38 g	Cholesterol: 0 g	Sodium: 234 mg

MEXICAN PIZZA

4 10-inch flour tortillas (substitute 6 6-inch flour
   tortillas if you can't find the larger size)
2 cups frozen corn kernels, thawed
2 medium ripe tomatoes, diced
1 medium green bell pepper, thinly sliced
4-ounce can chopped mild green chilies
1 to 1½ cups pre-grated reduced-fat cheddar cheese or
   cheddar-style soy cheese

1. Preheat the oven to 400 degrees.

2. Arrange the tortillas on two baking sheets that have
been lightly oiled or sprayed with vegetable oil cooking
spray.

3. Combine the corn, tomatoes, bell pepper slices, and
green chilies in a mixing bowl and toss together. Divide
the mixture among the tortillas, spreading evenly over the
entire surface to the edges.

4. Sprinkle the pizzas with the cheese, dividing it among
them evenly.

5. Bake for 4 to 5 minutes, or until the cheese is thoroughly melted. Let stand for 5 minutes, then cut each
into 6 wedges to serve.

Helpful tip: You might want to bake two pizzas at a time
(or three if you are using the smaller tortillas), and bake
the other two a few minutes later to use as second helpings.

Calories: 194	Total fat: 5 g	Protein: 9 g
Carbohydrate: 26 g	Cholesterol: 14 g	Sodium: 254 mg

Pantry staples
❑ Extra-virgin olive oil
❑ Black beans, 3 1-pound cans
❑ Onion, 1 large
❑ Ground cumin
❑ Dried oregano
❑ Chopped green chilies, mild,
   4-ounce can

Refrigerator staples
❑ Fresh garlic
❑ Lemon, 1

Freezer staples
❑ Corn kernels, 10-ounce package or
   portion of 1-pound bag

*Shopping list: fresh foods and
   nonstaples*
❑ Fresh parsley, 1 small bunch
❑ Green bell pepper, 1 medium
❑ Fresh tomatoes, 2 medium
❑ Pre-grated reduced-fat cheddar
   cheese, 8-ounce package, or
   cheddar-style soy cheese, 8 ounces
❑ 10-inch flour tortillas (or 6-inch
   flour tortillas), 1 package
❑ Reduced-fat sour cream, low-fat
   yogurt, or soy yogurt, 1-pint
   container
❑ Scallions, 1 bunch
❑ Salad ingredients as desired (if
   following menu suggestion, buy
   dark green lettuce, precut broccoli
   florets, cucumbers, and toasted
   sunflower or pumpkin seeds)

Chapter Three

GOING WITH THE GRAIN...
AND THE BEAN

Grains and beans are the mainstays of a sound meatless diet. Rich in vitamins and minerals, they are also excellent low-fat, high-fiber protein sources. Though the theory that grain and bean proteins must be combined in the same meal to be fully usable has been downplayed, they are undoubtedly a perfect culinary complement to one another. In the cuisines of cultures not so heavily dependent on meat, classic dishes abound that combine grains and beans.

Once regarded as "poor man's food," these staples have become downright trendy. Whether vegetarian or not, everyone seems interested in increasing their intake of this dynamic duo in their diet. But if you're often in a hurry to get food on the table and think you can't take advantage of traditionally long-cooking grains and beans, this chapter provides a solution. When dinner has to be on the table quickly, short-cuts *do* have to be taken, and it's better to take them, we think, rather than shy away from these nourishing foods.

With that in mind, you'll find a selection of hearty menus based on canned beans and convenient grains such as quick-cooking brown rice, now available in nearly every supermarket. Plus, you'll be introduced to quick dishes featuring couscous, bulgur, quinoa, and kasha.

Oriental Fried Rice
Spicy Zucchini
Cherry tomatoes

Fruit-and-Spice Couscous Pilaf
Creamed Curried Vegetables
Cucumber Raita
Prepared spicy chutney (optional)

Quinoa Pilaf with Peas and Almonds
Quick-Braised Fennel or Celery Hearts
Tossed Salad with Pinto Beans and Jicama

Rice with Black Beans and Chili-Cheese
Greens with Avocado and Pears
Fat-free tortilla chips

Lemon-Dill Rice
Hummus
Greek Salad
Warm pita breads

Curried Chickpea Stew
Green Rice
Tossed salad

Rice and Oriental Vegetable Medley
Spiced Diced Tofu

Hopping-John (Black-Eyed Peas with Rice)
Simple Green Salad with Corn and Tomatoes
Microwaved sweet potatoes

Kasha Varnishkes
Baby Lima Beans with Fennel and Walnuts
Fresh fruit

Kasha and Orzo Pilaf
Endive and Orange Salad
Multigrain bread

Bulgur with Cabbage and Onions
Black Bean Salad with Peppers and Feta Cheese
Tomato wedges

Bulgur with Sweet-and-Sour Vegetables
Cucumber and Watercress Salad

Black-Eyed Peas with Garlic and Thyme
Pepper and Tomato Medley
Fresh corn-on-the-cob
Whole-grain bread or rolls

Stir-Fried Vegetables with Couscous
Creamy Oriental Salad

MENU

Oriental Fried Rice

Spicy Zucchini

Cherry tomatoes

Serves 6

Tender grains of brown rice share the spotlight with crunchy vegetable bits and ribbons of egg pancake. Savory yet mellow at the same time, this dish is made even more appealing by contrasting it with spiced zucchini.

Strategy:

1. Prepare the Oriental Fried Rice.

2. Prepare the Spicy Zucchini.

3. Wash and stem some cherry tomatoes to serve alongside.

ORIENTAL FRIED RICE

6-serving portion quick-cooking brown rice
2 tablespoons canola oil
2 cups thinly sliced Chinese cabbage (thinly sliced celery may be substituted)
6- or 8-ounce can sliced water chestnuts, drained
1 small onion, halved and thinly sliced
10-ounce package (2 cups) frozen green peas, thawed
Freshly ground pepper, to taste
2 to 3 tablespoons soy sauce, or to taste
Vegetable oil cooking spray
2 large eggs, beaten
1 bunch scallions, green and white parts, sliced

1. In a medium-sized saucepan, cook the rice following package directions. When it's done, remove it from the heat, fluff it with a fork, and cover until needed.

2. In the meantime, heat the oil in a wok or a large, nonstick skillet. Add the cabbage (or celery), water chestnuts, and onion. Stir-fry over high heat 3 to 4 minutes only. Add the rice and the peas and mix well. Stir-fry over high heat for another 2 to 3 minutes. Season to taste with the pepper and soy sauce. Remove the wok or skillet from the heat and cover.

3. Spray another skillet with the cooking oil spray and heat. When the skillet is hot, add the eggs and cook without stirring, as if for a pancake, until the top is dry. Do not turn it. Remove the fried egg to a cutting board, cut it into narrow strips, and scatter it over the fried rice, followed by the scallions. Cover until needed and serve from the wok or skillet. Pass around a bottle of soy sauce for anyone who wishes to add more.

Variation: To make this an even more substantial dish, add ½ pound of diced firm tofu or baked pressed tofu.

Calories: 344	Total fat: 7 g	Protein: 10 g
Carbohydrate: 58 g	Cholesterol: 71 g	Sodium: 461 mg

SPICY ZUCCHINI

2 pounds small zucchini
2 tablespoons soy sauce, or to taste
2 tablespoons dark sesame oil
2 tablespoons apple juice
1½ teaspoons vegetarian Worcestershire sauce
1 tablespoon honey or brown rice syrup
2 cloves garlic, minced (optional)
1-inch piece unpeeled fresh ginger, minced, or
    ¼ teaspoon ground ginger
½ teaspoon dried red-pepper flakes or 1 teaspoon
    chili powder
1 scallion, thinly sliced, green part only

1. Wash and trim the zucchini, then cut into ¼-inch slices. Steam in a wide skillet with a small amount of water, covered, for 5 minutes.

2. In the meantime, combine the remaining ingredients in a small bowl and whisk together.

3. Combine the steamed zucchini and sauce in a serving bowl. Toss gently to coat the zucchini with sauce. Serve hot or at room temperature.

Calories: 80	Total fat: 5 g	Protein: 2 g
Carbohydrate: 8 g	Cholesterol: 0 g	Sodium: 354 mg

Pantry staples
❑ Canola oil
❑ Onion, 1 small
❑ Soy sauce
❑ Dark sesame oil
❑ Vegetarian Worcestershire sauce
❑ Honey or brown rice syrup
❑ Dried red-pepper flakes
❑ Quick-cooking brown rice
❑ Vegetable oil cooking oil spray

Refrigerator staples
❑ Eggs, 2 large
❑ Fresh garlic (optional)

Freezer staples
❑ Frozen green peas, 10-ounce package

Shopping list: fresh foods and nonstaples
❑ Small zucchini, 2½ pounds
❑ Fresh ginger
❑ Chinese cabbage, 1 small head
❑ Sliced water chestnuts, 6- or 8-ounce can
❑ Scallions, 1 bunch
❑ Apple juice, or frozen apple juice concentrate

MENU

Fruit-and-Spice Couscous Pilaf

Creamed Curried Vegetables

Cucumber Raita

Prepared spicy chutney (optional)

Serves 4 to 6

A curry feast in less than 30 minutes? Keep things simple and yes, it can be done. You'll be sure to make this meal of lovely flavors and textures a standard if you enjoy curries.

Strategy:

1. Prepare the carrots and potatoes for the Creamed Curried Vegetables and begin cooking them as directed in step 1 of the recipe.

2. Do steps 1 through 3 of the pilaf recipe.

3. Add the broccoli and peas to the carrot-potato mixture, then prepare the sauce for the curried vegetables.

4. Complete the pilaf recipe.

5. Complete the curried vegetables recipe.

6. At odd moments, put together the Cucumber Raita.

FRUIT-AND-SPICE COUSCOUS PILAF

Couscous (presteamed, cracked semolina) is a great grain for the busy cook. It need only be soaked in hot water for 10 to 15 minutes and it's done. These fine grains have the mild, familiar flavor of pasta — and no wonder, since semolina is the same durum wheat from which pasta is made. Both refined and whole wheat couscous are readily available at natural food stores. Use whichever you prefer.

1 cup raw couscous
2 tablespoons soy margarine
1 medium onion, finely chopped
2 medium apples, any variety, peeled and diced
½ cup chopped mixed dried fruits (see Note)
1 teaspoon cinnamon
½ teaspoon ground ginger
½ teaspoon turmeric
Salt, to taste
⅓ cup toasted sliced or slivered almonds

1. Combine the couscous in a heat-proof dish with 2 cups of boiling water. Cover and let stand 10 to 15 minutes, then fluff with a fork.

2. In the meantime, heat the margarine in a large skillet. Sauté the onion for 3 to 4 minutes over moderate heat, or until translucent.

3. Put the apple dice on top of the onions in the skillet, cover, and sauté for another 3 to 4 minutes, or until the apple has softened. Stir the apple-onion mixture, then stir the dried fruits into the skillet.

4. Stir the spices into ½ cup warm water. When the couscous is done, transfer it to the skillet along with the spice mixture. Stir well and cook for another 1 to 2 minutes, just until the mixture is well blended and heated through.

5. Add salt to taste, stir in the almonds, and serve.

Note: Packages of chopped mixed dried fruits are readily available in the dried fruit section of most supermarkets as well as in natural food stores.

Calories: 273	Total fat: 9 g	Protein: 5 g
Carbohydrate: 42 g	Cholesterol: 0 g	Sodium: 63 mg

CREAMED CURRIED VEGETABLES

Using jalapeño peppers in this dish gives it a fiery kick, but it is equally pleasing without them, as a mildly curried melange of vegetables.

2 large carrots, roughly chopped
2 medium potatoes, scrubbed and cut into large dice
3 cups precut broccoli florets
1 cup frozen green peas
2 tablespoons unbleached flour
¾ cup low-fat milk or soy milk
1 to 2 teaspoons good-quality curry powder, to taste
1 to 2 tablespoons minced fresh or bottled jalapeño
    pepper (optional)
Salt, to taste

1. Place the carrots and potatoes in a large, deep saucepan with enough water to cover all but about an inch of their volume. Bring to a simmer, cover, and cook until nearly tender, about 10 minutes.

2. Add the broccoli and frozen peas. Cover and cook another 5 minutes or so, or until the broccoli is tender-crisp and the peas are thawed.

Menu continues...

Pantry staples
❏ Onion, 1 medium
❏ Potatoes, 2 medium
❏ Cinnamon
❏ Ground ginger
❏ Turmeric
❏ Unbleached flour
❏ Curry powder

Refrigerator staples
❏ Soy margarine
❏ Low-fat milk or soy milk
❏ Carrots, 2 large
❏ Low-fat yogurt, plain, 8-ounce
    container

Freezer staples
❏ Frozen green peas, portion of
    10-ounce box or 1-pound bag

*Shopping list: fresh foods and
    nonstaples*
❏ Couscous, small box, or about
    ½ pound if bought in bulk
❏ Apples, 2 medium
❏ Mixed chopped dried fruit, 1 small
    package or small quantity
    purchased by weight
❏ Sliced or slivered almonds, small
    package
❏ Precut broccoli florets, about ½
    pound
❏ 1 fresh jalapeño pepper or 1 small
    jar chopped jalapeños (optional)
❏ Cucumber, 1 large
❏ Prepared spicy chutney (optional)

3. In the meantime, dissolve the flour in the milk or soy milk, then stir in the curry powder. Add the mixture to the vegetables, followed by the optional jalapeño pepper. Cook, uncovered, another 2 to 3 minutes, or until the liquid has thickened. Season to taste with salt. Serve with chutney on the side, if desired.

| Calories: 141 | Total fat: 1 g | Protein: 5 g |
| Carbohydrate: 28 g | Cholesterol: 2 g | Sodium: 78 mg |

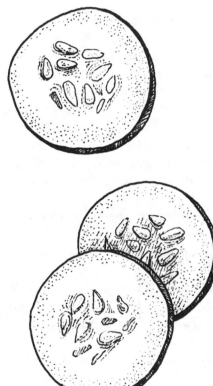

CUCUMBER RAITA

Here's a pared-down version of an already simple, palate-cooling relish traditionally served with curries.

1 large cucumber, peeled, quartered lengthwise, and diced
1 cup plain, low-fat yogurt
Salt and freshly ground pepper, to taste

1. If the cucumber seeds are small, they need not be removed, but if they are large and watery, remove them before dicing the cucumber.

2. Combine the cucumbers and yogurt in a serving dish and mix thoroughly. Season to taste with salt and pepper.

| Calories: 40 | Total fat: 1 g | Protein: 3 g |
| Carbohydrate: 5 g | Cholesterol: 3 g | Sodium: 37 mg |

QUINOA PILAF WITH PEAS AND ALMONDS

This simple pilaf makes for a good introduction to quinoa, if you're unfamiliar with it. See also Aztec Platter, page 176, in chapter 6, Salad Days.

1½ cups raw quinoa
3 to 4 scallions, white and green parts, thinly sliced
2 teaspoons salt-free herb-and-spice seasoning blend
1½ cups frozen green peas, thawed
2 tablespoons butter or soy margarine
Salt, to taste
⅓ cup slivered or sliced almonds

1. Bring 3 cups of water to a boil in a large, heavy saucepan. Rinse the quinoa well in a fine sieve. Stir the quinoa into the boiling water along with the scallions and seasoning blend. Cover and cook at a gentle but steady simmer until all the water has been absorbed, about 15 minutes.

2. Stir in the peas and margarine, then season to taste with salt. Transfer the pilaf to a serving bowl and scatter the almonds over the top. If time allows, you might like to lightly toast the almonds, either in a dry skillet over medium heat or in a 250-degree toaster oven. Watch carefully — they toast quickly!

Calories: 322	Total fat: 12 g	Protein: 11 g
Carbohydrate: 13 g	Cholesterol: 13 g	Sodium: 8 mg

Menu continues...

Menu continues...

MENU

Quinoa Pilaf with Peas and Almonds

Quick-Braised Fennel or Celery Hearts

Tossed Salad with Pinto Beans and Jicama

Serves 4 to 6

Quinoa is a quick grain with an ancient history. Known as the staple food of the ancient Aztecs, it is native to the South American Andes and is now also grown in the American Rockies. Quinoa has been steadily gaining in popularity in the natural food scene and is available at any natural food store, packaged in small boxes. Nutritionally, this is a powerhouse grain, high in protein and dense in a multitude of nutrients. For the hurried cook, quinoa is a pleasure — it cooks in 15 minutes to a light, fluffy texture.

Strategy:

1. Rinse the quinoa and begin cooking it as directed in step 1 of the pilaf recipe.

2. While the quinoa is cooking, prepare the Quick-Braised Fennel.

Strategy, continued

3. Complete the quinoa recipe.

4. Prepare the Tossed Salad with Pinto Beans and Jicama during odd moments of preparation of the other two recipes.

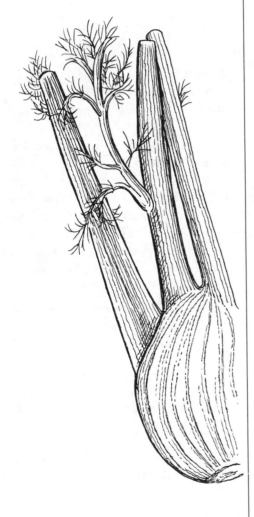

QUICK-BRAISED FENNEL OR CELERY HEARTS

Fennel is an anise-flavored vegetable that somewhat resembles celery. Out of season it tends to be a bit expensive, so we have recommended celery hearts as a substitute. Freeze the stalks and leaves trimmed from the fennel bulb, if desired, to add a touch of anise flavor to soups and stews you make at a future time.

3 large fennel bulbs (or substitute 1 package celery hearts)
1 tablespoon olive oil
2 medium garlic cloves, minced
1 tablespoon apple cider vinegar
Salt and freshly ground pepper, to taste
3 tablespoons minced fresh parsley

1. Trim the stalks and leaves away from the fennel bulbs, then slice them crosswise thinly, discarding the stem ends. If using celery hearts, slice them thinly on the diagonal. If you leave the stem end intact and use a sharp knife, you can slice through them all at once, making a quick job of it. Transfer the sliced fennel or celery to a colander and rinse.

2. Heat the oil in a large, heavy saucepan or deep, wide skillet. Add the garlic and sauté over low heat, stirring frequently for a minute or two, until lightly golden.

3. Add the sliced fennel or celery, the vinegar, and ½ cup water. Cover and cook over medium heat until tender-crisp, about 5 to 6 minutes. Season with salt and several good grinds of pepper. Transfer to a serving bowl, sprinkle parsley on top, and serve.

Calories: 38	Total fat: 2 g	Protein: 0 g
Carbohydrate: 3 g	Cholesterol: 0 g	Sodium: 65 mg

TOSSED SALAD WITH PINTO BEANS AND JICAMA

1 medium jicama (if unavailable, substitute 2 medium
    crisp white turnips), peeled and diced
1 cup canned pinto beans, drained and rinsed
1 medium red or green bell pepper, diced
½ pint cherry tomatoes
2 tablespoons minced fresh dill (optional)
Red or green leaf lettuce, as desired, torn
Reduced-fat bottled red-wine vinegar and oil salad
    dressing

1. Combine all the ingredients except the dressing in a
large salad bowl and toss well. Add a small amount of the
dressing or pass it around for everyone to dress their own.

Calories: 74	Total fat: 0 g	Protein: 3 g
Carbohydrate: 14 g	Cholesterol: 0 g	Sodium: 85 mg

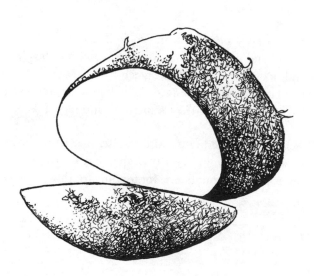

Pantry staples
❑ Olive oil
❑ Pinto beans, portion of 1-pound
    can
❑ Apple cider vinegar
❑ Salt-free herb-and-spice seasoning
    blend

Refrigerator staples
❑ Butter or soy margarine
❑ Fresh garlic

Freezer staples
❑ Frozen green peas, portion of
    10-ounce package or 1-pound bag

*Shopping list: fresh foods and
    nonstaples*
❑ Quinoa, 12-ounce box
❑ Scallions, 1 bunch
❑ Slivered or sliced almonds, small
    quantity
❑ Fennel, 3 large bulbs, or 1 package
    celery hearts
❑ Parsley, 1 small bunch
❑ Jicama, 1 medium, or white
    turnips, 2 medium
❑ Bell pepper, red or green,
    1 medium
❑ Cherry tomatoes, 1 pint
❑ Leaf lettuce, green or red,
    1 medium head
❑ Fresh dill (optional)
❑ Reduced-fat red-wine vinegar and
    oil salad dressing

MENU

Rice with Black Beans and Chili-Cheese

Greens with Avocado and Pears

Fat-free tortilla chips

6 to 8 servings

Rice and beans together make for a quick stick-to-the-ribs dish that will keep you feeling satisfied for a long time. Made with quick-cooking brown rice, this one-dish meal can be on the table in just 22 minutes.

Strategy:

1. Preheat the oven to 400 degrees. Prepare the Rice with Black Beans and Chili-Cheese. Place it in the oven and set the timer for 10 minutes.

2. Prepare the salad while the rice dish bakes.

RICE WITH BLACK BEANS AND CHILI-CHEESE

6-serving portion quick-cooking brown rice
3 cloves garlic, crushed and minced
1 large onion, chopped
1 tablespoon olive oil (optional)
1-pound can black beans, drained and rinsed
4-ounce can chopped mild green chilies
4 ounces pre-grated reduced-fat cheddar cheese
15-ounce container part-skim ricotta cheese
Chunky salsa for topping (optional)

1. Preheat the oven to 400 degrees. Lightly oil a 1½-quart baking dish.

2. Prepare the rice according to package directions. If desired, while the rice cooks, briefly sauté the garlic and onion in a tablespoon of olive oil until golden. But if you like the stronger flavor of uncooked onion and garlic, you can skip this step.

3. In a large bowl, mix the cooked rice with the beans, garlic, and onion. In another dish, combine the cheddar and ricotta cheeses with the green chilies. Layer half of the rice and bean mixture into the baking dish, followed by half of the cheddar-ricotta mixture, and repeat.

4. Bake the casserole 15 minutes. Remove from the oven, let stand for a minute or two, then cut into squares and serve, passing around salsa for topping for those who want it.

Calories: 429	Total fat: 12 g	Protein: 22 g
Carbohydrate: 55 g	Cholesterol: 37 g	Sodium: 235 mg

GREENS WITH AVOCADO AND PEARS

1 small head romaine or curly green or red leaf lettuce
Juice of ½ lemon
2 ripe, firm pears, such as Bosc or Bartlett
1 large ripe, firm avocado, preferably Haas
Bottled reduced-fat or fat-free poppy seed dressing, or
    other honey-sweetened salad dressing

1. Shred the lettuce and divide it among 6 or 8 salad plates.

2. Fill a large bowl with cold water and add the lemon juice; set aside. Peel the pears and cut them in half, then into quarters. With a small spoon or paring knife cut away the core and fibrous stem, immediately dropping the pear sections into the lemon water.

3. Halve the avocado; remove the large pit by sinking the blade of a knife into it and twisting it free. Peel each avocado half and drop it into the lemon water.

4. Slice the pears and avocado, and arrange them on the greens. Drizzle the salad lightly with bottled dressing, and serve immediately.

Calories: 107	Total fat: 4 g	Protein: 1 g
Carbohydrate: 16 g	Cholesterol: 0 g	Sodium: 4 mg

Pantry staples
- ❑ Quick-cooking brown rice
- ❑ Black beans, 1-pound can
- ❑ Onion, 1 large
- ❑ Chopped mild green chilies, 4-ounce can
- ❑ Olive oil (optional)

Refrigerator staples
- ❑ Lemon, 1
- ❑ Fresh garlic

Shopping list: fresh foods and nonstaples
- ❑ Romaine or curly green or red leaf lettuce, 1 small head
- ❑ Avocado, 1 firm ripe, preferably Haas
- ❑ Pears, 2 firm ripe, Bosc or Bartlett
- ❑ Ricotta cheese, part-skim, 15-ounce container
- ❑ Pre-grated reduced-fat cheddar cheese, 8-ounce package
- ❑ Poppy seed dressing, or other honey-sweetened salad dressing
- ❑ Chunky salsa, mild to hot as preferred (optional)
- ❑ Tortilla chips, preferably fat-free

MENU

Lemon-Dill Rice

Hummus

Greek Salad

Warm pita breads

Serves 6 to 8

This thoroughly satisfying meal with a Greek flair features a myriad of textures, flavors, and colors. You'll be pleasantly surprised at how quickly the three components can be put together. And since you'll need to have only one burner on for a brief time, this is a great choice for a warm-weather meal.

Strategy:

1. Cook the rice according to package directions.

2. While it cooks, prepare the Hummus.

3. Finish preparing the rice dish, cover, and set aside.

4. Place 6 to 8 foil-wrapped pitas in a 250-degree oven or toaster oven to warm. Before serving, cut them into halves or quarters.

5. Make the Greek Salad.

LEMON-DILL RICE

6-serving portion quick-cooking brown rice
1 tablespoon soy margarine or olive oil
Juice of 1 lemon
¼ cup chopped fresh dill
1 scallion, minced
Salt and freshly ground pepper, to taste

1. Cook the rice following package directions.

2. When it's done, stir in the remaining ingredients, cover, and set aside until needed.

Calories: 147	Total fat: 4 g	Protein: 3 g
Carbohydrate: 28 g	Cholesterol: 0 g	Sodium: 1 mg

HUMMUS

This classic Middle Eastern dip is meant to be scooped up with warm pita bread. Tahini, or sesame paste, is essential to its characteristic flavor and is readily available at natural food stores.

1-pound can chickpeas, drained and rinsed
¼ cup tahini (sesame paste)
¼ cup water, or as needed
1 clove garlic, crushed, or ½ teaspoon garlic powder
Juice of 1 lemon
½ teaspoon ground cumin
Salt and freshly ground pepper, to taste
Paprika for garnish

1. Combine all the ingredients except the last 2 in the container of a food processor. Process until smoothly blended, adding small amounts of water if necessary. The consistency should be that of a thick dip.

2. While the mixture is still in the processor, season it to taste with salt and pepper, pulsing the processor on and off to mix. Transfer the mixture to a serving bowl and dust the top with paprika.

Calories: 133	Total fat: 5 g	Protein: 5 g
Carbohydrate: 16 g	Cholesterol: 0 g	Sodium: 132 mg

GREEK SALAD

1 medium cucumber, peeled and sliced
1 medium green or red bell pepper, cut into strips
2 large tomatoes, diced
1 cup thinly shredded red cabbage
½ cup cured black olives
1 small red onion, thinly sliced
4 to 6 ounces crumbled feta cheese
Dark green lettuce leaves as needed, torn
Dried oregano
Olive oil
Red-wine vinegar

1. In a large salad bowl, combine the first 8 ingredients and toss well.

2. Sprinkle the salad with dried oregano, and pass around separate cruets of olive oil and vinegar for everyone to dress their salads to their taste.

Calories: 116	Total fat: 8 g	Protein: 4 g
Carbohydrate: 7 g	Cholesterol: 18 g	Sodium: 305 mg

Pantry staples
❏ Quick-cooking brown rice
❏ Olive oil
❏ Red-wine vinegar
❏ Dried oregano
❏ Paprika
❏ Chickpeas, 1-pound can
❏ Ground cumin
❏ Garlic powder (if not using fresh)

Refrigerator staples
❏ Soy margarine
❏ Lemons, 2
❏ Fresh garlic

Shopping list: fresh foods and nonstaples
❏ Fresh dill, 1 bunch
❏ Cucumber, 1 medium
❏ Green or red bell pepper, 1 medium
❏ Tomatoes, 2 large
❏ Scallions, 1 bunch
❏ Red cabbage, 1 small
❏ Red onion, 1 small
❏ Dark green lettuce
❏ Feta cheese, 4 to 6 ounces
❏ Cured black olives, about 4 ounces
❏ Tahini (sesame paste), small container
❏ Pita breads, 1 or 2 packages of 6

MENU

Curried Chickpea Stew

Green Rice

Tossed salad

Serves 6 to 8

Canned chickpeas are surely one of the most satisfactory of all canned vegetables. If you want to cook them from scratch, by all means do so. Cover them with cold water, bring to a boil, and cook for 2 minutes. Let them soak, covered, for 1 hour, then drain, cover with fresh water, bring to a simmer, and cook slowly 1 to 2 hours, or until tender. Be sure to buy your dried chickpeas in a health or natural foods store, since the ones sold in supermarkets tend to be too old. If a chickpea has celebrated its first birthday, it's not likely ever to become tender again.

Strategy:

1. Prepare the Curried Chickpea Stew through step 1.

2. Cook the rice according to package directions.

3. Continue step 2 of the stew.

4. Process the herbs and greens and toss with the cooked rice.

3. Prepare a simple tossed salad.

CURRIED CHICKPEA STEW

2 tablespoons olive oil
1 medium onion, chopped
1 medium green bell pepper, diced
2 1-pound cans chickpeas, drained and rinsed
4 large cloves garlic, crushed and minced
2 teaspoons good-quality curry powder, or to taste
14-ounce can imported plum tomatoes
with liquid, chopped
2 10-ounce packages frozen chopped spinach,
thawed and squeezed
Salt, to taste

1. Heat the olive oil in a soup pot. Add the onion and green pepper and cook over medium-high heat, stirring occasionally, for 4 minutes. Add the chickpeas, garlic, curry powder, and ½ cup water. Bring to a simmer and cook for 5 minutes, covered.

2. Stir in the tomatoes with their liquid and the chopped spinach, and season with salt to taste. Cover and cook for 10 minutes more. Serve in bowls or over the green rice.

| Calories: 232 | Total fat: 5 g | Protein: 9 g |
| Carbohydrate: 35 g | Cholesterol: 0 g | Sodium: 337 mg |

GREEN RICE

8-serving portion quick-cooking brown rice
1 to 1½ cups parsley leaves (about 1
   good-sized bunch)
¾ cup coarsely chopped scallions
2 tablespoons melted butter or margarine
½ teaspoon salt, or to taste
¼ teaspoon white pepper, or to taste

1. Cook the rice according to package directions.

2. In the meantime, trim the larger stems from the parsley, but don't be too fussy about the small ones. Combine them with the scallions in a food processor fitted with a steel blade and process until minced.

3. Combine the parsley-scallion mixture with the hot cooked rice in the saucepan, add butter or margarine, and salt and pepper to taste. Fluff with a fork, reheat for a minute, and serve.

Calories: 207	Total fat: 4 g	Protein: 4 g
Carbohydrate: 38 g	Cholesterol: 9 g	Sodium: 6 mg

Pantry staples
❏ Plum tomatoes, 14-ounce can
❏ Chickpeas, 2 1-pound cans
❏ Onion, 1 medium
❏ Quick-cooking brown rice
❏ Olive oil
❏ Curry powder, good-quality
❏ White pepper

Refrigerator staples
❏ Fresh garlic
❏ Butter or margarine

*Shopping list: fresh foods and
   nonstaples*
❏ Frozen chopped spinach, 2
   10-ounce packages
❏ Parsley, 1 large bunch
❏ Scallions, 1 bunch
❏ Green bell pepper, 1 medium
❏ Salad ingredients of your choice

MENU

Rice and Oriental Vegetable Medley

Spiced Diced Tofu

Serves 4 to 6

Stir-fries can sometimes involve a fair amount of work, especially if there are a lot of vegetables to chop. But don't be intimidated by the long list of ingredients in this one; most of the vegetables simply get tossed into the wok with little or no cutting needed. This is an attractive dish of colorful vegetables and nuts mounded over hot rice; the spicy bites of tofu served on the side add just the right finishing touch.

Strategy:

1. Prepare the Spiced Diced Tofu through step 2.

2. Prepare the Rice and Oriental Vegetable Medley.

3. Finish the last step of the Spiced Diced Tofu.

RICE AND ORIENTAL VEGETABLE MEDLEY

6-serving portion quick-cooking brown rice
1 tablespoon canola or safflower oil
1 teaspoon dark sesame oil
1 tablespoon soy sauce
¼ cup dry red wine or sherry
4 cups precut broccoli florets
2 medium carrots, sliced diagonally, ½ inch thick
1 large red bell pepper, cut into 1-inch dice
1 cup small whole white mushrooms
1 cup canned baby corn or trimmed fresh snow peas
6- to 8-ounce can water chestnuts or bamboo shoots, drained, liquid reserved
1½ tablespoons cornstarch
¼ cup sliced almonds or chopped toasted cashews for topping

1. Cook the rice according to package directions. When it's done, fluff it with a fork and cover until needed.

2. In a wok or large soup pot, heat the oils, soy sauce, and wine or sherry, then stir in the broccoli and carrots. Cover and steam the vegetable mixture over medium-high heat for 4 to 5 minutes.

3. Add the red pepper, mushrooms, baby corn or snow peas, and water chestnuts or bamboo shoots. Stir-fry over medium-high heat for 5 minutes, or until all the vegetables are brightly colored and tender-crisp.

4. Dissolve the cornstarch in the liquid reserved from the water chestnuts or bamboo shoots. Add enough water to the mixture to equal 1 cup of liquid. Add it to the skillet and cook another 2 to 3 minutes, or until thickened.

5. Spread the rice over the bottom of a large round casserole dish or a large platter. Mound the vegetables over the rice, then sprinkle the almonds or cashews over the top. Serve at once, passing around extra soy sauce for anyone who wants it.

| Calories: 386 | Total fat: 8 g | Protein: 8 g |
| Carbohydrate: 65 g | Cholesterol: 0 g | Sodium: 269 mg |

SPICED DICED TOFU

1 pound firm tofu
1 tablespoon canola or safflower oil
1 to 2 tablespoons soy sauce, to taste
Paprika, to taste
Chili powder, to taste
2 scallions, sliced

1. Slice the tofu crosswise, ½ inch thick. Place the slices between paper towels or a clean tea towel and blot to remove excess moisture. Cut the tofu into ½-inch dice.

2. Heat the oil and soy sauce slowly in a nonstick skillet. Stir the tofu in quickly, then turn the heat up to moderately high. Cook, stirring frequently, until the tofu is browned and crisp on all sides, about 10 to 12 minutes.

3. Sprinkle with paprika and chili powder as desired, stir well, then stir in the scallions. Cook for about another minute, then remove from the heat and serve or cover until needed. Serve alongside the rice and vegetables.

| Calories: 97 | Total fat: 7 g | Protein: 7 g |
| Carbohydrate: 3 g | Cholesterol: 0 g | Sodium: 308 mg |

Pantry staples
❑ Quick-cooking brown rice
❑ Canola or safflower oil
❑ Dark sesame oil
❑ Dry red wine or sherry
❑ Soy sauce
❑ Cornstarch
❑ Paprika
❑ Chili powder

Refrigerator staples
❑ Carrots, 2 medium
❑ Scallions

Shopping list: fresh foods and nonstaples
❑ Precut broccoli florets, about ½ to ¾ pound
❑ Red bell pepper, 1 large
❑ Mushrooms, white, small, about ¼ pound
❑ Baby corn, 1-pound can, or fresh snow peas, about ¼ pound
❑ Water chestnuts or bamboo shoots, 6- to 8-ounce can
❑ Sliced almonds or chopped toasted cashews, small package
❑ Tofu, firm, 1-pound package

MENU

Hopping-John
(Black-Eyed Peas with Rice)

**Simple Green Salad with Corn and
Tomatoes**

Microwaved sweet potatoes

Serves 6

---

*This homey, Southern-style menu features
a vegetarian version of "Hopping John," a
classic dish of black-eyed peas and rice. Taking another cue from Southern tradition,
we've accompanied it with sweet potatoes —
these often overlooked vegetables are packed
with nutrients, especially valuable beta-
carotene. Besides, they're delicious, and their
wonderful flavor and color round out a
simple meal.*

Strategy:

1. Place 6 medium sweet potatoes in
    the microwave and cook for a mul-
    tiple of 3 to 4 minutes per potato,
    depending on the wattage of your
    unit. Tɪᴘ: If your microwave is less
    than 750 watts, you may want to
    bake 3 potatoes at a time, serve every-
    one half, then bake the other 3 to
    serve as a second helping. Otherwise,
    they may not be done in the allotted
    time.

2. Prepare the Hopping-John.

HOPPING-JOHN
(Black-Eyed Peas with Rice)

*This adaptation of a classic Deep South dish substitutes Cre-
ole-influenced flavorings for the meat that is traditionally used
as a "seasoning."*

6-serving portion quick-cooking brown rice
2 tablespoons safflower or canola oil
1 cup chopped onions
1 to 2 cloves garlic, minced
2 cups ripe, juicy tomatoes, diced, plus ¼ cup water,
    or 1 14-ounce can diced plum tomatoes with liquid
½ teaspoon dried basil
½ teaspoon dried thyme
1-pound can black-eyed peas, drained and rinsed
Salt and freshly ground black pepper, to taste

1. Cook the rice following package directions.

2. Heat the oil in a very large skillet. Sauté the onion over
moderate heat until translucent, about 4 minutes, then
add the garlic and continue to sauté until the onion is
golden, another 4 to 5 minutes or so.

3. Add the tomatoes and herbs and cook the mixture for 3
to 4 minutes.

4. Add the cooked rice and black-eyed peas. Season to
taste with salt and lots of freshly ground pepper. Cover
and cook until well heated through, about 5 to 7 minutes.
Add a bit of water if the mixture needs more moisture.

Variation: For a spicy kick, pass around some Tabasco or
other hot sauce for anyone who might want it.

Calories: 275	Total fat: 6 g	Protein: 7 g
Carbohydrate: 48 g	Cholesterol: 0 g	Sodium: 8 mg

SIMPLE GREEN SALAD WITH CORN AND TOMATOES

Corn kernels add an unexpected flavor and nice color to a very simple salad. Dress this salad any way you'd like — with just a touch of olive oil and lemon juice or wine vinegar, or use a prepared dressing.

1 cup frozen corn kernels, thoroughly thawed
1 small red or green bell pepper, cut into strips
3 plum tomatoes, sliced
1 cup coarsely shredded red cabbage
Dark green lettuce, such as romaine, or red leaf
    lettuce, torn, as needed

1. Combine all the ingredients in a salad bowl and toss. Dress as desired.

Calories: 49	Total fat: 0 g	Protein: 2 g
Carbohydrate: 10 g	Cholesterol: 0 g	Sodium: 12 mg

Strategy, continued

3.   At odd moments during the preparation time, prepare the salad.

Pantry staples
❏ Quick-cooking brown rice
❏ Safflower or canola oil
❏ Onions, about 2 medium
❏ Plum tomatoes, 14-ounce can, if not using fresh
❏ Dried basil
❏ Dried thyme
❏ Tabasco sauce (optional)

Refrigerator staples
❏ Fresh garlic

Freezer staples
❏ Frozen corn kernels, portion of 10-ounce box or 1-pound bag

Shopping list: fresh foods and nonstaples
❏ Black-eyed peas, 1-pound can
❏ Tomatoes, ripe, juicy, about 1 pound
❏ Plum tomatoes, fresh, 3 medium
❏ Red or green bell pepper, 1 small
❏ Red cabbage
❏ Dark green lettuce, such as romaine, or red leaf lettuce
❏ Sweet potatoes, 6

MENU

Kasha Varnishkes

Baby Lima Beans with Fennel and Walnuts

Fresh fruit

Serves 6

Kasha, a.k.a. toasted buckwheat groats, is not a grain at all but a member of the rhubarb family. A groat is the kernel of the plant's seed pod. If untoasted, they're called buckwheat groats and are found only in health and natural food stores. Look for kasha in the Jewish foods section of supermarkets. They're available in three grinds — fine, medium, and coarse. If you've never eaten groats before, we recommend you start with the toasted medium grind.

Varnishkes is a traditional Russian-Jewish dish that combines kasha with noodles. The rich, unusual taste of this grain-that's-not-a-grain will appeal to those with more adventurous palates, who will understand immediately why it's been popular since the tenth century B.C.

Strategy:

1. Begin cooking the bowtie noodles for Kasha Varnishkes.

2. Cook the kasha and proceed with the rest of the recipe.

3. Prepare the Baby Lima Beans recipe.

KASHA VARNISHKES

2 cups uncooked bowtie pasta (farfelle)
1 teaspoon canola oil
1 medium onion, chopped (2 cups)
1-pound can vegetable broth
1 cup medium-grind kasha (buckwheat groats)
1 whole egg, or ¼ cup egg substitute
Salt and freshly ground pepper, to taste

1. Cook the bowtie pasta until *al dente*, about 12 minutes. Drain and set aside.

2. Heat the oil in a heavy saucepan. Add the onion and cook over medium-high heat, stirring occasionally, until golden, about 5 or 6 minutes. Add the vegetable broth, stir, and bring to a simmer.

3. In the meantime, stir the kasha and egg or egg substitute together in a medium-sized bowl. Transfer the mixture to a large heavy skillet, preferably cast iron, and place it over medium heat. Stir the kasha with a fork until the grains separate and become dry, about 3 minutes. Remove from the heat.

4. Slowly add the simmering onion and stock to the kasha, so that it doesn't boil up fast. Lower the heat to a simmer, cover, and cook over low heat 15 minutes. Uncover, fold in the cooked pasta, and season to taste with salt and pepper.

Calories: 264	Total fat: 3 g	Protein: 8 g
Carbohydrate: 51 g	Cholesterol: 36 g	Sodium: 219 mg

BABY LIMA BEANS WITH FENNEL AND WALNUTS

Showcased as a first course so that all the complex flavors and textures can be fully appreciated, or featured on the side as an accent, this dish is best served at room temperature.

2 10-ounce packages frozen baby lima beans
1 large shallot, finely chopped
1 tablespoon white-wine vinegar, or more
    or less to taste
½ teaspoon salt
1½ tablespoons canola oil
2 teaspoons dark sesame oil
1 tablespoon thick, plain low-fat yogurt
1 small fennel bulb (½ pound), quartered, cored,
    and sliced crosswise very thinly
1 tablespoon finely chopped fennel leaves
1 tablespoon finely chopped parsley
¼ cup coarsely chopped walnuts
¼ teaspoon white pepper

1. Cook the lima beans in a small amount of salted water for 5 minutes. Plunge them into cold water to stop the cooking process, drain, and transfer to a salad bowl.

2. In a small bowl, combine the shallot, vinegar, and salt. Whisk in the vegetable oil, sesame oil, and yogurt. Pour over the lima beans.

3. Add the remaining ingredients and toss gently. Taste and add more salt if desired.

Calories: 176	Total fat: 8 g	Protein: 7 g
Carbohydrate: 20 g	Cholesterol: 0 g	Sodium: 208 mg

Strategy, continued

4. At odd moments during the preparation time, prepare a simple presentation of fresh fruit, such as red grapes combined with pear slices or melons, depending on the season.

Pantry staples
❏ Canola oil
❏ White-wine vinegar
❏ Dark sesame oil
❏ Onion, 1 medium
❏ White pepper

Refrigerator staples
❏ Egg, 1 large, or ¼ cup egg substitute
❏ Plain low-fat yogurt, 8-ounce cup

Shopping list: fresh foods and nonstaples
❏ Medium-grind kasha (buckwheat groats), 13-ounce box
❏ Vegetable broth, 1-pound can
❏ Bowtie pasta, 1-pound package
❏ Frozen baby lima beans, 2 10-ounce packages
❏ Shallot, 1 large
❏ Fennel bulb, 1 small
❏ Parsley, 1 bunch
❏ Walnuts, chopped
❏ Fresh fruits (red grapes and pears or melons, or whatever fruits desired)

KASHA AND ORZO PILAF

MENU

Kasha and Orzo Pilaf

Endive and Orange Salad

Multigrain bread

Serves 4

A bit more sophisticated than the Kasha Varnishkes, this pilaf complements a sauté of seitan "steaks" beautifully (page 148), if you'd like to vary the menus, or works alone as a study in contrasting textures. A salad of curly endive and sweet seedless orange slices lends a refreshing flavor complement.

Strategy:

1. Prepare the Kasha and Orzo Pilaf.

2. Prepare the salad.

3. Slice purchased fresh multigrain bread and arrange on a plate.

KASHA AND ORZO PILAF

1 cup raw orzo (rice-shaped) pasta
1½ cups rich vegetable broth
1 cup raw kasha, medium grind
1 large egg, lightly beaten, or ¼ cup egg substitute
2 medium carrots, grated in food processor
2 teaspoons butter or soy margarine
½ teaspoon dried thyme
Salt, to taste
8 to 10 grinds fresh black pepper
½ cup minced parsley
2 scallions, white and green parts, thinly sliced

1. Cook the orzo in a large pot of boiling water until just *al dente*. Drain, rinse with cold water, and drain again.

2. In the meantime, bring the vegetable stock to a simmer in a small saucepan.

3. While the orzo cooks, combine the kasha and egg in a mixing bowl and stir well to coat each grain. In a large well-seasoned cast-iron or nonstick skillet over high heat, cook the egg-coated kasha, stirring constantly and scraping it up from the bottom, until the kernels are dry and separated and give off a nutty toasted aroma.

4. Slowly add the hot broth, stir well, and cover. Cook until the kasha is tender, about 15 minutes.

5. Stir in the carrots, butter, and thyme. Season to taste with salt and pepper, cover, and let stand off the heat for 3 minutes. Toss with the parsley and scallions and serve.

Calories: 227	Total fat: 5 g	Protein: 6 g
Carbohydrate: 39 g	Cholesterol: 59 g	Sodium: 179 mg

ENDIVE AND ORANGE SALAD

2 tablespoons olive oil
2 tablespoons apple cider vinegar
1 tablespoon undiluted orange juice concentrate
2 small seedless oranges, peeled and sectioned
½ cup very thinly sliced red onion
1 head curly endive, tough outer leaves discarded,
  chopped

1. Combine the oil, vinegar, and juice concentrate in a small bowl and stir together.

2. Slice or section the oranges, then place them in a salad bowl with the sliced onion and endive. Pour in the dressing and toss well.

Calories: 161	Total fat: 7 g	Protein: 2 g
Carbohydrate: 23 g	Cholesterol: 0 g	Sodium: 14 mg

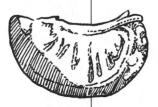

Pantry staples
❏ Dried thyme
❏ Olive oil
❏ Apple cider vinegar

Refrigerator staples
❏ Egg, 1 large, or ¼ cup egg substitute
❏ Carrots, 2 medium
❏ Butter or soy margarine

Freezer staples
❏ Orange juice concentrate

Shopping list: fresh foods and nonstaples
❏ Orzo (rice-shaped pasta), 1-pound box
❏ Vegetable broth, 1-pound can
❏ Kasha (buckwheat groats), medium grind, 13-ounce box
❏ Scallions, 1 bunch
❏ Curly endive, 1 small head
❏ Parsley, 1 bunch
❏ Seedless Temple or navel oranges, or tangelos, 3
❏ Red onion, 1 small
❏ Multigrain bread, 1 loaf

MENU

Bulgur with Cabbage and Onions

Black Bean Salad with Peppers and Feta Cheese

Tomato wedges

Serves 6

This simple yet robust meal perfectly fits the profile of the ideal grain-and-bean combo — it's filling, high in fiber, and low in fat. You might like to top this off with a light, sweet dessert such as Pineapple-Yogurt Ambrosia (page 192).

Strategy:

1. Do steps 1 and 2 of Bulgur with Cabbage and Onions.

2. In the meantime, prepare the Black Bean Salad.

3. Complete the bulgur recipe.

4. Cut the tomato wedges.

BULGUR WITH CABBAGE AND ONIONS

Bulgur is presteamed, cracked wheat and has a nutty, hearty flavor. Traditionally, it is cooked by pouring boiling water over it and letting it stand for about 30 minutes; however, there's no law against simmering it, in which case it's ready in 15 minutes, making it a great, quick-cooking grain. You'll find bulgur in any natural food store.

1 cup raw bulgur
2 tablespoons canola or safflower oil
1 large yellow or red onion, quartered and thinly sliced
8-ounce package pre-shredded coleslaw cabbage
  (see Note)
1 tablespoon poppy seeds
Salt and freshly ground pepper, to taste

1. Bring 2 cups of water to a boil in a large, heavy saucepan. Stir in the bulgur, then cover and cook at a gentle but steady simmer until the water is absorbed, about 15 minutes.

2. Heat the oil in a large skillet. Add the onion, then, without mixing, layer the shredded cabbage over it. Cover and sauté over moderate heat for 5 minutes.

3. Stir the onion-cabbage mixture together, then cover and sauté for another 5 minutes, or until the onion and cabbage are wilted.

4. When the bulgur is done, fluff it with a fork, then transfer it to the skillet, stirring it into the onion-cabbage mixture. Stir in the poppy seeds and season to taste with lots of salt and freshly ground pepper. Cover until needed.

Note: Of course, half of a 1-pound bag of pre-shredded coleslaw cabbage may also be used. Using a brand that includes thin shreds of carrot adds a nice touch to this dish.

| Calories: 183 | Total fat: 5 g | Protein: 5 g |
| Carbohydrate: 29 g | Cholesterol: 0 g | Sodium: 11 mg |

BLACK BEAN SALAD WITH PEPPERS AND FETA CHEESE

2 1-pound cans black beans, rinsed and drained
1 small green bell pepper, sliced
1 small red bell pepper, sliced
2 scallions, minced
4 ounces feta cheese, crumbled
1 tablespoon extra-virgin olive oil
Juice of ½ to 1 lemon, to taste
Freshly ground pepper, to taste
Curly lettuce leaves (optional)

1. Combine all of the ingredients except the lettuce in a serving bowl and mix gently but thoroughly. If desired, place each serving on a curly lettuce leaf.

| Calories: 229 | Total fat: 7 g | Protein: 12 g |
| Carbohydrate: 30 g | Cholesterol: 17 g | Sodium: 213 mg |

Pantry staples
❏ Canola or safflower oil
❏ Onion, 1 large, yellow or red
❏ Poppy seeds
❏ Black beans, 2 1-pound cans
❏ Extra-virgin olive oil

Refrigerator staples
❏ Lemon, 1

Shopping list: fresh foods and nonstaples
❏ Bulgur, small box, or about ½ pound if bought in bulk
❏ Pre-shredded coleslaw cabbage, 8-ounce bag, or portion of 1-pound bag
❏ Green bell pepper, 1 small
❏ Red bell pepper, 1 small
❏ Feta cheese, 8-ounce package
❏ Tomatoes, 3 large or 6 plum
❏ Scallions, 1 bunch
❏ Curly green leaf lettuce (optional)

Bulgur with Sweet-and-Sour
Vegetables

Cucumber and Watercress Salad

Serves 6

---

*The savory flavors of vegetables and tofu
contrasted with the sweetness of pineapple
make for a winning combination. Together
with a salad that pairs soothing cucumber
with the peppery flavor of watercress, this
memorable meal looks and tastes as if a lot
more time and effort went into it than actually did.*

Strategy:

1. Prepare the Bulgur with Sweet-and-
   Sour Vegetables.

2. At odd moments of the preparation
   time, prepare the Cucumber and
   Watercress Salad.

BULGUR WITH SWEET-AND-SOUR VEGETABLES

1½ cups bulgur (presteamed, cracked wheat)
1½ tablespoons canola oil
1 medium onion, chopped
1 medium red bell pepper, cut into 1-inch dice
1 medium green bell pepper, cut into 1-inch dice
1 medium zucchini, quartered lengthwise, then cut
   into ½-inch chunks
14-ounce can plum tomatoes, chopped, with liquid
1-pound can pineapple chunks in unsweetened juice,
   drained, juice reserved
8-ounce package baked pressed tofu or 8 ounces extra-
   firm tofu, diced

Sauce
Reserved pineapple juice
2 tablespoons soy sauce
3 tablespoons rice vinegar or white-wine vinegar
2 tablespoons honey or brown rice syrup
2 tablespoons cornstarch

**Dry-roasted peanuts or toasted cashews for topping
   (optional)**

1. Bring 3 cups of water to a boil in a large saucepan (for
even better flavor, replace part of the water with canned
vegetable stock). Stir in the bulgur and simmer, covered,
for about 15 minutes, or until the water is absorbed. When
the bulgur is done, fluff it with a fork and remove from
the heat.

2. Heat the oil in a large skillet or wok. Add the onion and
sauté over medium-high heat, covered, until limp, about
3 to 4 minutes. Add the peppers and zucchini and sauté,
covered, another 5 minutes, stirring occasionally. Stir in
the tomatoes, pineapple chunks, and diced tofu.

3. Combine the ingredients for the sauce in a small bowl and stir until the cornstarch has dissolved. Pour the sauce into the skillet, bring it to a simmer, and cook at a steady simmer for another 5 minutes. Taste, and if needed, adjust the sweet-sour balance with more honey and/or vinegar.

4. Serve at once over the cooked bulgur, topping each serving with a small amount of peanuts or cashews, if desired.

| Calories: 286 | Total fat: 4 g | Protein: 9 g |
| Carbohydrate: 45 g | Cholesterol: 0 g | Sodium: 350 mg |

CUCUMBER AND WATERCRESS SALAD

2 medium cucumbers, peeled and sliced
½ bunch watercress, leaves and stems, chopped
¾ cup plain, low-fat yogurt or reduced-fat sour cream
Salt, to taste

1. Combine all of the ingredients in a serving bowl. Toss well to mix.

| Calories: 34 | Total fat: 1 g | Protein: 2 g |
| Carbohydrate: 5 g | Cholesterol: 5 g | Sodium: 27 mg |

Pantry staples
- ❑ Canola oil
- ❑ Onion, 1 medium
- ❑ Plum tomatoes with liquid, 14-ounce can
- ❑ Soy sauce
- ❑ Rice vinegar or white-wine vinegar
- ❑ Honey or brown rice syrup
- ❑ Cornstarch

Shopping list: fresh foods and nonstaples
- ❑ Bulgur, small box, or about ½ pound if bought in bulk
- ❑ Red bell pepper, 1 medium
- ❑ Green bell pepper, 1 medium
- ❑ Zucchini, 1 medium
- ❑ Baked pressed tofu, 8-ounce package, or extra-firm tofu, 8 ounces
- ❑ Pineapple chunks in unsweetened juice, 1-pound can
- ❑ Dry-roasted peanuts or toasted cashews
- ❑ Cucumbers, 2 medium
- ❑ Watercress, 1 bunch
- ❑ Yogurt, plain, low-fat, or reduced-fat sour cream

MENU

Black-Eyed Peas with Garlic and Thyme

Pepper and Tomato Medley

Fresh corn-on-the-cob

Whole-grain bread or rolls

Serves 6

Keep a variety of canned beans in your pantry and you'll always be halfway toward a myriad of quick, delicious dishes. This main dish of black-eyed peas is a particular favorite. Spiked with garlic and aromatic thyme, it needs only the simplest of accompaniments to complete the meal.

Strategy:

1. Begin cooking the corn-on-the-cob in a large pot, allowing one ear per serving. Or if you prefer, prepare the corn and place in a microwavable dish and microwave it instead. You need to use at least a 750-watt unit to make sure the 6 ears of corn will be ready in the allotted time.

2. Prepare the Black-Eyed Peas with Garlic and Thyme.

3. Prepare the Pepper and Tomato Medley.

BLACK-EYED PEAS WITH GARLIC AND THYME

3 1-pound cans black-eyed peas, drained and rinsed
2 to 4 cloves garlic, finely minced
3 sprigs fresh thyme, or 1 teaspoon dried thyme
1 tablespoon olive oil
Salt and freshly ground pepper, to taste
¼ cup finely chopped fresh parsley or fresh dill, or more or less, to taste

1. In a medium saucepan, combine drained peas, garlic, thyme, and oil, plus 1 cup of water. Bring to a boil, then reduce the heat and simmer, covered, for 10 minutes.

2. Uncover, season with salt and pepper, and allow to stand uncovered until needed. Just before serving, stir in the parsley or dill. Serve in small bowls.

Calories: 223	Total fat: 4 g	Protein: 12 g
Carbohydrate: 37 g	Cholesterol: 0 g	Sodium: 8 mg

PEPPER AND TOMATO MEDLEY

3 large green bell peppers, cut in 2-inch squares
6 Roma or plum tomatoes, cut into large chunks
½ cup small pitted black olives
2 tablespoons olive oil
Juice of ½ lemon
Salt and freshly ground pepper, to taste
2 tablespoons minced fresh parsley

1. In a medium-sized serving bowl, combine the bell peppers, tomatoes, and olives.

2. In a small bowl, stir together the oil and lemon juice. Pour this dressing over the vegetables. Season with salt and pepper to taste and sprinkle with parsley.

Calories: 95	Total fat: 7 g	Protein: 1 g
Carbohydrate: 7 g	Cholesterol: 0 g	Sodium: 96 mg

Pantry staples
❏ Olive oil
❏ Black olives, small pitted, 8-ounce can or portion of 1-pound can

Refrigerator staples
❏ Lemon, 1
❏ Fresh garlic

Shopping list: fresh foods and nonstaples
❏ Black-eyed peas, 3 1-pound cans
❏ Fresh or dried thyme
❏ Parsley, 1 bunch
❏ Fresh dill, 1 small bunch
❏ Green bell peppers, 3 large
❏ Roma or plum tomatoes, 6
❏ Corn-on-the-cob, 6 ears
❏ Whole-grain bread or rolls

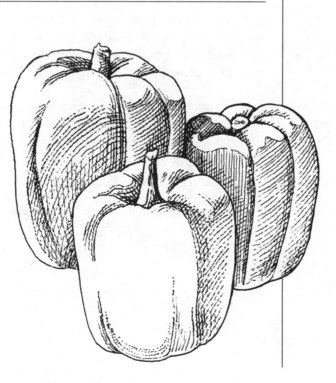

Stir-Fried Vegetables with Couscous

Creamy Oriental Salad

Serves 6

Quick, where's the protein? In the case of this offbeat, Oriental-flavored meal, it's hidden in the creamy salad dressing, composed of tofu and tahini. Combining quick-cooking couscous with frozen stir-fried vegetables makes for a grain dish that practically prepares itself, so that you can fully attend to the true centerpiece of this meal, which is the salad.

Strategy:

1. Prepare the Stir-Fried Vegetables with Couscous through step 2.

2. Prepare the Creamy Oriental Salad.

3. Finish the last step of the stir-fried vegetable recipe.

STIR-FRIED VEGETABLES WITH COUSCOUS

We hope you've already become acquainted with couscous earlier in this chapter. If not, you only need to know that this fluffy, light grain with the taste of pasta is presteamed, cracked semolina (the heart of durum wheat) and is available at any natural food store and in most supermarkets.

1¼ cups raw couscous
1 tablespoon dark sesame oil
2 tablespoons soy sauce
¼ cup dry red wine or sherry
1-pound bag frozen Oriental stir-fry vegetables (unseasoned), thawed

1. Combine the couscous with 2½ cups boiling water in a heat-proof container. Cover tightly and let stand until all the water has been absorbed, about 10 to 15 minutes. Fluff with a fork.

2. Combine the oil, soy sauce, and wine or sherry in a very large skillet or wok. Add the vegetables and cook over moderately high heat for about 8 minutes, or until all the vegetables are well heated through and brightly colored.

3. Stir the cooked couscous together with the vegetables. Cook for another 2 to 3 minutes, then remove from the heat and keep covered until needed. Pass around extra soy sauce for anyone who may want it.

Calories: 102	Total fat: 2 g	Protein: 3 g
Carbohydrate: 14 g	Cholesterol: 0 g	Sodium: 350 mg

CREAMY ORIENTAL SALAD

With crunchy vegetables enveloped in a creamy dressing, this salad offers an unusual mix of lively flavors and textures.

8-ounce package fresh mung bean sprouts
3 stalks bok choy or celery, trimmed of leaves and
    sliced diagonally
2 medium carrots, sliced diagonally
1 medium red bell pepper, cut into long strips

Dressing
½ pound soft tofu or firm silken tofu
¼ cup tahini (sesame paste) or peanut butter
1 scallion, chopped
¼ cup rice vinegar or white-wine vinegar
2 teaspoons honey or brown rice syrup
½ teaspoon grated fresh ginger, or ¼ teaspoon
    ground ginger
½ teaspoon salt

1. Steam the bean sprouts in a deep, heavy saucepan with an inch or so of water for 2 to 3 minutes, covered, or until just wilted. Stir once or twice during that time. Transfer to a colander and rinse with cold water until cool; let drain while preparing the other vegetables.

2. Combine the remaining vegetables in a serving bowl. Stir in the sprouts.

3. Combine the dressing ingredients in a food processor fitted with a steel blade. Process until completely smooth. You will need to drizzle in from 2 to 4 tablespoons of water, depending on the type of tofu used, to make the dressing more fluid.

4. Pour the dressing over the salad and toss well.

Calories: 131	Total fat: 6 g	Protein: 6 g
Carbohydrate: 11 g	Cholesterol: 0 g	Sodium: 226 mg

Pantry staples
❑ Dark sesame oil
❑ Soy sauce
❑ Dry red wine or sherry
❑ Rice vinegar or white-wine vinegar
❑ Honey or brown rice syrup
❑ Ground ginger (or grated fresh)
❑ Peanut butter (optional, to be used if tahini isn't)

Refrigerator staples
❑ Carrots, 2 medium

Shopping list: fresh foods and nonstaples
❑ Frozen Oriental stir-fry vegetables (unseasoned), 1-pound bag
❑ Couscous, about ½ pound
❑ Mung bean sprouts, fresh, 8-ounce bag
❑ Bok choy or celery
❑ Red bell pepper, 1 medium
❑ Scallions
❑ Tofu, soft, ½ pound, or portion of 10-ounce package silken tofu
❑ Tahini (sesame paste)
❑ Fresh ginger (or ground ginger may be substituted)

Chapter Four

PIZZAS, SANDWICHES, AND BURGERS

At first glance, you might think that this chapter is one of compromises and letdowns. If you want pizza, why not call the pizza parlor? And everyone settles for sandwiches for supper from time to time — out of desperation, right? Well, don't go away, because we would venture to say that this is one of the chapters we had the most fun with. With a bit of ingenuity, a pizza, sandwich, or burger supper can be anything but boring.

Why make pizza? Simply because you can stretch your definition of what pizza is, going way beyond tomato sauce and tons of cheese. Using prebaked pizza shells, pitas, or Italian bread as the base, creative and tasty homemade pizzas are just minutes away. Sandwiches for supper can offer many pleasant surprises as well, and are especially satisfying when teamed with quick soups, as we have done in several of the menus that follow. Finally, you'll find a small sampling of hearty, bean-based burgers so filling in and of themselves that they need only the simplest of accompaniments to complete the meal.

Pizza à la Niçoise
Green Salad with Tomatoes, Cannellini, and Zucchini

New York Reuben Pizza
Simple tossed salad
Orange Cream Flip

Broiled Veggie Pizza
Broccoli Slaw

Pesto Pizza with Fresh Tomatoes
Mixed greens with vinaigrette

Pita Pizzas, Plain and Fancy
Cruciferous Crunch Salad

Spicy Black Bean Burgers in Pita Pockets
Fresh Tomato Salsa
Corn-on-the-cob
Fat-free tortilla chips

Chickpea Burgers in Sesame Seed Rolls
Creamy Coleslaw
Vegetable medley

Pinto Bean Sloppy Joes
Zucchini-Broccoli Relish Salad
Microwaved potatoes or sweet potatoes

White Bean Pâté
Crispbreads, crackers, and fresh breads
Olives and cherry tomatoes
Fresh fruit and cheese plate

Chunky Bean Spread
Refreshingly Fruited Red Cabbage Salad
Corn-on-the-cob

Mozzarella in Carrozza
Cucumber Salad
Cool Tomato Cream Soup

Quick Pasta and Bean Soup
Vegetable Hero
Small seedless oranges

Farmhouse Creamed Corn Soup
Black Olive Tapenade Pita Rolls
Roasted Asparagus with Sesame Seeds

Eggless "Egg Salad" Pitas
Mushroom Broth with Rice and Snow Peas
Half-sour dill pickle spears and tomato wedges

Vegetable Rarebit
Greens with Oranges and Sweet Vinaigrette
Steamed broccoli

Gazpacho
Dilled Tofu Spread
Dark rye or pumpernickel bread, or fresh bagels

MENU

Pizza à la Niçoise

Green Salad with Cannellini, Tomatoes, and Zucchini

Serves 4 to 6

The Italian border is a mere 20-minute train ride from the French city of Nice, where pizza is every bit as popular as it is in Italy. This classic is called a "white pizza" because its components don't include tomatoes or a red sauce. Instead, it's smothered with sautéed onions and then topped with tiny black olives, rosemary, and Parmesan cheese. The contrast of onions, subdued into sweetness, with the sharp tang of well-brined olives couldn't be more appealing.

The pizza can be made any time of year, but teamed with a hearty cannellini salad with ripe tomatoes, zucchini, and fresh herbs, this becomes a splendid summer meal, so long as it's not too hot to turn on your oven.

Strategy:

1. Prepare the pizza and place it in the oven. Set the timer for 10 minutes.

2. While it bakes, prepare the salad.

PIZZA À LA NIÇOISE

Use the tiny olives called niçoise if available, or Greek black olives such as Kalamata.

1½ tablespoons olive oil
4 large onions, sliced
½ cup niçoise or Greek olives, pitted and chopped
2 12-inch prebaked pizza crusts or 1 long, large loaf French or Italian bread, cut in half horizontally
A sprinkling of dried or fresh rosemary, to taste
⅓ cup grated Parmesan cheese, preferably fresh, or soy Parmesan

1. Preheat oven to 425 degrees.

2. Heat the oil in a nonstick skillet, and sauté the onions over medium heat, covered. Lift the lid to stir often, until tender and lightly browned, about 10 minutes.

3. While the onions cook, pit and chop the olives.

4. Spread the onions over the pizza shells or divide them between the 2 halves of French or Italian bread. Top with olives, rosemary, and Parmesan cheese. Bake 10 minutes, or until the top and crust are golden. Cut the pizzas into wedges or sections and serve.

| Calories: 302 | Total fat: 8 g | Protein: 10 g |
| Carbohydrate: 46 g | Cholesterol: 4 g | Sodium: 550 mg |

GREEN SALAD WITH CANNELLINI, TOMATOES, AND ZUCCHINI

1-pound can cannellini (great Northern beans),
　　drained and rinsed
1 pound ripe tomatoes, cut into large dice
1 medium zucchini, sliced
1 medium red bell pepper, cut into strips
2 tablespoons chopped fresh basil (in season)
¼ cup chopped fresh parsley
Dark green lettuce leaves, as needed
Olive oil
Red-wine vinegar

1. Combine all the salad ingredients except the oil and vinegar in a serving bowl and toss. Drizzle with the oil and vinegar and toss again.

| Calories: 139 | Total fat: 2 g | Protein: 6 g |
| Carbohydrate: 21 g | Cholesterol: 0 g | Sodium: 191 mg |

Pantry staples
❏ Olive oil
❏ Dried rosemary (or substitute fresh if available)
❏ Onions, 4 large
❏ Red-wine vinegar
❏ Cannellini (great Northern beans), 1-pound can

Refrigerator staples
❏ Grated Parmesan cheese or soy Parmesan

Shopping list: fresh foods and nonstaples
❏ 2 12-inch prebaked pizza crusts, or 1 long, large loaf French or Italian bread
❏ Niçoise olives or Greek olives, about ¼ pound
❏ Tomatoes, 1 pound
❏ Zucchini, 1 medium
❏ Red bell pepper, 1 medium
❏ Fresh basil (in season), 1 small bunch
❏ Fresh parsley, 1 small bunch
❏ Dark green lettuce, such as romaine

MENU

New York Reuben Pizza

Simple tossed salad

Orange Cream Flip

Serves 4 to 6

If you think about it, it's not the bread that makes a Reuben sandwich so good, it's the filling. You can transfer all of that goodness (sans meat, of course), to a French bread pizza, and it's still a juicy, flavorful experience.

Strategy:

1. Preheat the oven to 425 degrees.

2. Prepare the Reuben pizzas and place them in the oven. Set the timer for 10 minutes.

3. Prepare a simple tossed salad with greens, tomatoes, other vegetables, and a dressing of your choice.

4. Blend or process the ingredients for Orange Cream Flip.

5. Remove the pizzas from the oven, let them stand for a minute or two, then cut them into sections and serve.

NEW YORK REUBEN PIZZA

Baked tofu, a savory, pressed variety available in 8-ounce packages in most natural food stores, makes a wonderful substitute for the meat found in traditional Reubens.

3 tablespoons ketchup
½ cup reduced-fat mayonnaise or commercially prepared tofu mayonnaise
2 tablespoons sweet pickle relish, well drained
1 long loaf French bread
2 tablespoons brown or Dijon mustard
1-pound can sauerkraut, very well drained
1 small red onion, halved and thinly sliced (optional)
8-ounce package baked tofu, cut into ½-inch dice
6 to 8 thin slices aged Swiss cheese
Kosher dill pickle spears for garnish

1. Preheat the oven to 425 degrees.

2. Combine the ketchup, mayonnaise, and pickle relish in a small bowl and stir until well blended.

3. Cut the French bread in half horizontally, and take a thin slice off the rounded half, if necessary, so that it will sit firmly on the baking sheet. Hollow out the soft centers, leaving a 1-inch shell all around.

4. Layer the Reubens as follows: Spread each bread hollow with the ketchup-mayonnaise mixture, then place a ribbon of mustard down the center. Spread a mound of well-drained sauerkraut on each, followed by the red onion, if desire, then the cubed tofu. Top each pizza with 3 to 4 slices of Swiss cheese.

5. Bake for 10 minutes, or until the cheese is bubbly. Remove the Reuben pizzas from the oven, let them stand a minute or two, then cut each pizza into sections. Serve at once, with kosher pickle spears on the side.

Variation: For a nondairy version, use thin slices of mozzarella-style soy cheese instead of Swiss cheese.

Helpful tip: Wrap the soft bread centers and freeze them for using when soft bread crumbs are called for.

Calories: 332	Total fat: 13 g	Protein: 13 g
Carbohydrate: 35 g	Cholesterol: 19 g	Sodium: 1023 mg

ORANGE CREAM FLIP

This smooth beverage makes an uncommonly tasty pizza dinner even better.

1 quart orange juice
1 pint frozen low-fat vanilla yogurt or nondairy frozen
    dessert

1. In a blender, combine the orange juice and vanilla yogurt; process until smooth and frothy. Pour the mixture into glasses and serve at once with straws.

Calories: 173	Total fat: 1 g	Protein: 6 g
Carbohydrate: 35 g	Cholesterol: 5 g	Sodium: 67 mg

Refrigerator staples
❑ Reduced-fat mayonnaise or commercially prepared tofu mayonnaise
❑ Ketchup
❑ Brown or Dijon mustard

Shopping list: fresh foods and nonstaples
❑ French bread, 1 long loaf
❑ Sweet pickle relish, 1 small jar
❑ Red onion, 1 small (optional)
❑ Aged Swiss cheese, sliced, small package
❑ Sauerkraut, 1-pound can
❑ Baked tofu, 8-ounce package
❑ Salad greens and vegetables of your choice
❑ Kosher dill pickle spears
❑ Orange juice, 1 quart
❑ Frozen low-fat vanilla yogurt or nondairy frozen dessert, 1 pint

MENU

Broiled Veggie Pizza

Broccoli Slaw

Serves 4 to 6

Broiling or grilling vegetables does something truly remarkable to the way they taste: the natural sugars respond to the "caramelizing" that takes place over high heat, giving the natural goodness an even deeper taste that's sweeter and richer. It's so addictive, you might find yourself preparing vegetables this way frequently.

Strategy:

1. Preheat the oven's broiler.

2. Cut the vegetables for the Broiled Veggie Pizza and broil them.

3. Lower the oven heat to 425 degrees.

4. Assemble the pizzas and place them in the oven; set the timer for 10 minutes.

5. Prepare the Broccoli Slaw.

BROILED VEGGIE PIZZA

1 large eggplant (1½ pounds), unpeeled, sliced lengthwise ¼ inch thick
3 medium zucchini, unpeeled, sliced lengthwise ¼ inch thick
2 medium green bell peppers, cut into strips
Olive oil cooking spray
3 large ripe firm tomatoes, sliced
2 to 3 large cloves garlic, sliced
½ cup pitted black olives
2 large prebaked pizza shells, or 2 long loaves French bread
2 teaspoons dried Italian herb seasoning mix, or to taste
Salt and freshly ground pepper, to taste
½ cup grated Parmesan cheese

1. Preheat the oven's broiler. Line a baking sheet with aluminum foil.

2. If using French bread, cut it horizontally, trimming the rounded half, if necessary, to ensure it will sit firmly on the baking sheet.

3. Spray the eggplant and zucchini slices and the green pepper strips on both sides with the cooking oil spray, and place them in a single layer on the baking sheet; broil 2 to 3 minutes, turn and broil another 2 minutes. Cut the eggplant and zucchini into large chunks.

4. Reset the oven to 425 degrees. Layer the tomato slices, garlic, eggplant, zucchini, bell peppers, and black olives on the pizza shells or bread halves. Sprinkle with the Italian herbs, salt and pepper to taste, if desired, and Parmesan cheese. Bake 10 minutes.

5. Remove from the oven, let stand 1 to 2 minutes, then cut into wedges (or sections if using French bread) and serve hot.

Calories: 469	Total fat: 10 g	Protein: 20 g
Carbohydrate: 74 g	Cholesterol: 6 g	Sodium: 793 mg

BROCCOLI SLAW

1 large bunch broccoli
6 scallions, white and green parts, thinly sliced

Dressing
½ cup reduced-fat mayonnaise or commercially
    prepared tofu mayonnaise
½ cup plain low-fat yogurt
2 tablespoons Dijon-style mustard
2 teaspoons Italian herb seasoning mix
½ teaspoon dried red-pepper flakes (optional)

1. Cut the broccoli florets from the stalks. Peel the stalks and grate them coarsely, either with a hand grater or in a food processor fitted with a coarse grating disk. Slice the florets thinly.

2. Combine the broccoli and scallions in a serving bowl.

3. Combine the dressing ingredients in a small bowl and stir to mix well, then pour the dressing over the broccoli and toss together until well mixed.

Calories: 119	Total fat: 8 g	Protein: 3 g
Carbohydrate: 9 g	Cholesterol: 10 g	Sodium: 357 mg

Pantry staples
Olive oil cooking spray
Dried Italian herb seasoning mix
Dried red-pepper flakes (optional)
Black olives, pitted, 8-ounce can, or
    portion of 1-pound can

Refrigerator staples
Fresh garlic
Reduced-fat mayonnaise or
    commercially prepared tofu
    mayonnaise
Plain low-fat yogurt
Grated Parmesan cheese
Dijon-style mustard

*Shopping list: fresh foods and
    nonstaples*
Eggplant, 1 (about 1½ pounds)
Zucchini, 3 medium
Green bell peppers, 2 medium
Ripe firm tomatoes, 3 large
Broccoli, 1 large bunch
Scallions, 1 bunch
Prebaked pizza shells, 2 large, or
    French bread, 2 long loaves

MENU

Pesto Pizza with Fresh Tomatoes

Mixed greens with vinaigrette

Serves 6

Thanks to the pesto sauce, this pizza comes with plenty of built-in flavor. There's no need to do anything more than prepare a simple salad of seasonal greens, then serve and wait for the compliments.

Strategy:

1. Preheat the oven to 425 degrees.

2. Make the pesto; assemble the pizzas and place them in the oven. Set the timer for 10 minutes.

3. Prepare a simple salad of mixed lettuces, perhaps contrasting tender Boston or Bibb lettuce with the deeper green of romaine or chicory. Add some carrot and red cabbage shreds, plus some sliced Belgian endive or bok choy. Serve with cruets of olive oil and vinegar.

4. Check the pizzas and set the timer for another 2 to 4 minutes, if necessary, or until the mozzarella cheese looks bubbly and golden brown.

PESTO PIZZA WITH FRESH TOMATOES

This pesto base omits all the oil and Parmesan cheese traditional to it, for a result that is much lower in fat.

Light and simple pesto sauce
1 large bunch fresh basil, tough stems removed
½ cup parsley leaves
½ cup walnuts, toasted pine nuts, or toasted almonds
Juice of ½ lemon

2 12-inch prebaked pizza shells
4 to 6 large, ripe but firm tomatoes, thinly sliced
2 cups pre-grated part-skim mozzarella cheese, or
    2 cups grated mozzarella-style soy cheese

1. Preheat the oven to 425 degrees.

2. Combine the ingredients for the pesto in a food processor. Process until finely chopped. Drizzle in some water until the mixture has the consistency of a thick paste.

3. Spread the pesto sauce evenly over the pizza shells. Arrange the tomatoes in overlapping rows around the outside of the shells, then another row inside the first, then another until the surface is completely covered.

4. Sprinkle the surface with the mozzarella cheese and place the pizzas in the oven. Set the timer for 10 minutes. Bake 10 minutes, then check to see if the bottom is crisp and the cheese is golden brown. If not quite ready, bake for another 2 to 4 minutes. Let the pizzas stand for a minute or so, then cut them into wedges to serve.

Variation: Out of basil season, you can use bottled pesto sauce that is readily available in specialty shops and some supermarkets.

Calories: 396	Total fat: 14 g	Protein: 20 g
Carbohydrate: 44 g	Cholesterol: 26 g	Sodium: 582 mg

Pantry staples
- ❑ Olive or canola oil (for salad)
- ❑ Red-wine or cider vinegar (for salad)

Refrigerator staples
- ❑ Lemon, 1

Shopping list: fresh foods and nonstaples
- ❑ Basil, 1 large bunch
- ❑ Prebaked pizza shells, 2 12-inch
- ❑ Tomatoes, firm ripe, 4 to 6 medium
- ❑ Parsley, 1 small bunch
- ❑ Walnuts, toasted pine nuts, or toasted almonds, small quantity
- ❑ Pre-grated part-skim mozzarella cheese, 8-ounce package, or mozzarella-style soy cheese, 8 ounces
- ❑ Salad greens as suggested

Pita Pizzas, Plain and Fancy

MENU

Pita Pizzas, Plain and Fancy

Cruciferous Crunch Salad

Serves 6 or more

Here's a carefree menu that can be varied in many ways according to your mood. Put away those measuring cups and let your creative spirit take over while creating any number of simple but special minipizzas. The Cruciferous Crunch Salad featuring raw broccoli and red cabbage (two members of the cruciferous vegetable family proven to have so many healthful benefits) seems to complement any of these pizza possibilities splendidly.

Strategy:

1. Preheat the oven to 400 degrees and spray a baking sheet or two, as needed, with vegetable oil cooking spray.

2. Assemble the pizzas with the toppings of your choice.

3. While the pizzas are baking, make the salad.

PITA PIZZAS, PLAIN AND FANCY

With this flexible recipe, you can make the number of pizzas you need at any given time. For the most part, one generously topped pita pizza should be allowed per serving, but those with heartier appetites might be able to handle two. As we said before, don't worry about measuring, simply top the pizzas as you'd like.

For each of the suggested pizzas below, start by preheating your oven to 400 degrees and spraying a baking sheet or two, as needed, with vegetable oil cooking spray.

Basic Pita Pizza with Toppings

This is all you need to make a basic pita pizza, and chances are that kids will prefer this pared-down version over anything fancier!

Pita breads, preferably whole-grain
Italian canned crushed or pureed tomatoes
Pre-grated part-skim mozzarella cheese, or mozzarella-style soy cheese, grated
Dried oregano

1. Spread each pita with a good layer of crushed or pureed tomatoes and top with mozzarella cheese and a sprinkling of dried oregano. If desired, add one of the following toppings (or create your own) before baking. Arrange pitas on a baking sheet and bake for 10 minutes.

The following analysis is based on using ⅓ cup part-skim Mozzarella per pita:

Calories: 240	Total fat: 5 g	Protein: 14 g
Carbohydrate: 32 g	Cholesterol: 16 g	Sodium: 470 mg

Toppings:

Not really pepperoni: Scatter thin slices of tofu hot dog over the cheese.

Florentine: Scatter thawed, frozen chopped spinach, well drained, over the cheese.

The Greek: Scatter thawed, frozen chopped spinach over the tomato sauce, and top with crumbled feta cheese instead of mozzarella.

Puttanesca: Top the pizza with chopped black and green olives.

The classic: Top the pizza with sautéed sliced mushrooms and bell pepper strips.

If you want to get a little fancier (but by no means more complicated), here are two other possibilities:

Broccoli and Red Onion White Pita Pizza

Olive oil
Sliced red onion
Chopped broccoli florets
Pita breads, preferably whole-grain
Part-skim ricotta cheese
Pre-grated part-skim mozzarella cheese

1. Heat a small amount of olive oil as needed in a skillet over moderately high heat. Sauté the onion until translucent, then add some broccoli florets, turn the heat down to moderate, cover, and cook for 3 to 5 minutes, or until the broccoli is tender-crisp.

2. Spread the pitas with a thin, even layer of ricotta cheese, followed by a sprinkling of mozzarella cheese, then the onion-broccoli mixture. Arrange the pitas on a baking sheet and bake for 10 minutes.

The following analysis is based on using ¼ cup each of part-skim mozzarella and ricotta per pita:

Calories: 379	Total fat: 12 g	Protein: 23 g
Carbohydrate: 42 g	Cholesterol: 35 g	Sodium: 557 mg

Pantry staples
- ❏ Crushed or pureed canned tomatoes, as needed
- ❏ Light olive oil (optional for salad)
- ❏ Red-wine vinegar (optional for salad)

Shopping list: fresh foods and nonstaples
- ❏ Pita breads, 1 to 2 packages of 6
- ❏ Romaine lettuce, 1 medium head
- ❏ Broccoli, 1 small bunch
- ❏ Red cabbage, 1 small head
- ❏ Cherry tomatoes, 1 pint
- ❏ Dry-roasted sunflower seeds, small quantity
- ❏ Ingredients as needed for whatever type of pita pizzas you are preparing

Red Pepper and Goat Cheese Pita Pizza

Fresh or canned, drained, plum tomatoes, sliced
Pita breads, preferably whole-grain
Bottled roasted red bell peppers, cut into strips
Crumbly goat cheese such as Montrachet
Dried thyme

1. Arrange tomato slices on the pitas, then top with strips of roasted peppers and goat cheese. Sprinkle dried thyme over the top. Arrange the pitas on baking sheets and bake for 8 to 10 minutes.

The following analysis is based on using 2 tablespoons of goat cheese and ¼ cup of red pepper per pita:

Calories: 267	Total fat: 7 g	Protein: 12 g
Carbohydrate: 38 g	Cholesterol: 25 g	Sodium: 652 mg

CRUCIFEROUS CRUNCH SALAD

Dress this satisfying green salad with a splash of olive oil and red-wine vinegar, or a prepared salad dressing of your choice.

½ medium head romaine lettuce, or as needed
1 small bunch broccoli, stems and florets, chopped, lightly steamed, if desired
1 cup thinly sliced red cabbage, or more if desired
½ pint halved cherry tomatoes
Olive oil and red-wine vinegar or dressing of your choice
Dry-roasted sunflower seeds

1. Combine the first 4 ingredients in a large salad bowl and toss. Dress as you wish, or let everyone dress their own salad. Top with a scattering of sunflower seeds.

Calories: 61	Total fat: 3 g	Protein: 1 g
Carbohydrate: 5 g	Cholesterol: 0 g	Sodium: 14 mg

SPICY BLACK BEAN BURGERS IN PITA POCKETS

Baking burgers rather than frying and flipping them adds up to a savings of time, effort, and of course, fat content. They won't be as crisp and brown as fried burgers, but the marvelous flavor and tasty toppings make up for that.

1 teaspoon olive oil
1 small onion, finely chopped
3 cloves garlic, minced
2 large scallions, white and green parts, sliced
4-ounce can diced green chilies, drained
2 plum tomatoes, seeded and diced
2 1-pound cans black beans, drained and rinsed
1 egg, beaten
¼ cup unbleached flour or potato starch
6 large pita breads, warmed in foil

Garnishes
Lettuce, finely shredded
Ripe tomatoes, finely diced
6 scallions, green and white, thinly sliced
Sliced black olives
Reduced-fat sour cream or yogurt
Pre-grated reduced-fat cheddar cheese (optional)
Fresh Tomato Salsa (recipe follows)

1. Preheat the oven to 375 degrees.

2. In a heavy skillet, heat the oil with a tablespoon of water and "sweat" the onion and garlic, covered, until the water evaporates and they turn golden. Stir in the scallions, chilies, and tomatoes. Remove from the heat.

3. Put the beans into the workbowl of a food processor fitted with a steel blade. Add the onion-garlic mixture followed by the egg and flour or potato starch and process until it is blended, with some chunky texture remaining.

MENU

Spicy Black Bean Burgers in Pita Pockets

Fresh Tomato Salsa

Corn-on-the-cob

Fat-free tortilla chips

Serves 6

This burger is my version of an upscale first course I enjoyed a few years ago in an award-winning Jacksonville café. I enjoyed it so much, in fact, that I immediately went home and began looking for a fast route to this dish, which the chef confided had taken him hours to prepare. The answer is, of course, to use canned black beans rather than dried. After that, it's just a matter of putting together all the aromatic and savory ingredients and popping it, juicy and hot, into pita bread.
— *L. K.*

Strategy:

1. Prepare the Spicy Black Bean Burgers through step 2.

2. Begin cooking the corn in a large cooking pot, allowing one ear per serving. Or if you prefer, microwave it.

3. Complete the recipe for the burgers and put them in the oven.

4. Prepare the salsa.

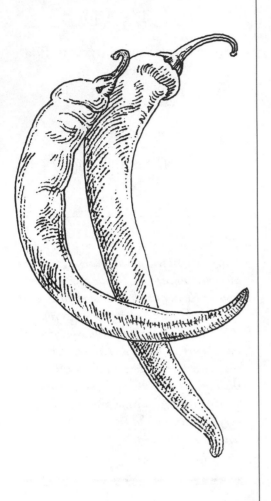

Menu continues...

4. Line a baking sheet with aluminum foil, then spray evenly with cooking oil spray. Divide the black bean batter evenly into 12 patties and arrange them on the baking sheet. Bake for 10 to 12 minutes, or until the patties are firm to the touch.

5. Remove the baking sheet from the oven, then very carefully, remove each patty with a wide spatula and transfer to a serving platter.

6. Let everyone prepare their own sandwiches as follows: Cut each pita bread in half to form two pockets. Carefully open each half and slide a hot patty into each. Pass around separate bowls of lettuce, diced tomato, scallions, black olives, sour cream or yogurt, shredded cheese, if desired, and Fresh Tomato Salsa (recipe follows), so that everyone can garnish their own sandwich. Serve with the tortilla chips and corn-on-the-cob.

The following analysis is based on 2 burgers per serving (without garnishes):

Calories: 232	Total fat: 4 g	Protein: 20 g
Carbohydrate: 42 g	Cholesterol: 18 g	Sodium: 296 mg

FRESH TOMATO SALSA

The salsas that are available in the supermarket these days are quite good, but you might like to try the homemade kind, especially during the summer when sun-ripened tomatoes are at hand. If tomatoes are out of season, however, use canned Italian plum tomatoes rather than resorting to the hothouse type.

5 large ripe but firm tomatoes, or 28-ounce can Italian
    plum tomatoes in puree
1 fresh jalapeño pepper, seeded and deveined
8-ounce can tomato sauce (omit if using canned
    tomatoes in puree)
1 medium onion, cut up
4 to 6 sprigs (depending on size) fresh parsley or
    cilantro
Salt, to taste (optional)

1. If using fresh tomatoes, core them over a bowl to catch and reserve the juices.

2. In a food processor fitted with a steel blade and with the motor running, drop the jalapeño pepper through the feed tube and process until finely minced. Add the tomatoes and their juices, tomato sauce (unless using canned tomatoes), onion, and parsley or cilantro. Pulse just a few times to make a medium-chunky consistency.

Calories: 42	Total fat: 0 g	Protein: 1 g
Carbohydrate: 9 g	Cholesterol: 0 g	Sodium: 297 mg

Pantry staples
❑ Olive oil
❑ Vegetable oil cooking spray
❑ Black beans, 2 1-pound cans
❑ Onions, 1 small and 1 medium
❑ Green chilies, chopped,
    4-ounce can
❑ Black olives, pitted, 8 ounce can or
    portion of 1-pound can
❑ Unbleached white flour or potato
    starch

Refrigerator staples
❑ Fresh garlic
❑ Egg, 1

*Shopping list: fresh foods and
    nonstaples*
❑ Plum tomatoes, 2 medium, plus
    extra if using for garnish
❑ Ripe tomatoes, 5 large, or Italian
    plum tomatoes in puree, 28-ounce
    can
❑ Pita bread, package of 6
❑ Lettuce, any type, 1 small head
❑ Scallions, 1 bunch
❑ Fresh parsley or cilantro, 1 small
    bunch
❑ Reduced-fat sour cream or yogurt,
    1-pint container
❑ Pre-grated reduced-fat cheddar
    cheese (optional)
❑ Tomato sauce, 8-ounce can
❑ Fresh jalapeño pepper, 1 small
❑ Corn-on-the-cob, 6 ears
❑ Fat-free tortilla chips, 8- or
    10-ounce bag

MENU

Chickpea Burgers in Sesame Seed Rolls

Creamy Coleslaw

Vegetable Medley

Serves 6

Dense with a rich nutty taste, these burgers are a lower-fat cousin of traditional Middle Eastern falafel. Like the black bean burgers in the previous menu, these are baked, not fried, making for a savings of effort and fat content. The addition of curry powder and chutney gives these burgers an East Indian flavor.
— L. K.

Strategy:

1. Prepare the Chickpea Burgers.

2. While the burgers bake, prepare the Creamy Coleslaw.

3. Cook a 1-pound bag of any of those interesting frozen mixed vegetable varieties available in supermarkets. Serve plain or with just a touch of butter or margarine for flavor.

4. Assemble the burgers and serve with the coleslaw and vegetables.

CHICKPEA BURGERS IN SESAME SEED ROLLS

2 scallions, coarsely chopped
¼ cup chopped fresh parsley, or more or less to taste
¼ cup walnuts
¼ cup wheat germ
2 1-pound cans chickpeas, drained and rinsed
1 teaspoon Madras or other good-quality curry powder
1 large egg and 1 egg white, ¼ cup egg substitute, or ¼ cup potato starch
6 large sesame seed burger or kaiser rolls

Garnishes
Curly endive or other lettuce
1 red onion, thinly sliced
Prepared chutney

1. Preheat the oven to 375 degrees.

2. In a food processor fitted with a steel blade, finely chop the scallions, parsley, walnuts, wheat germ, and chickpeas. Transfer the mixture to a bowl and stir in the curry powder, egg or egg substitute, or potato starch.

3. Line a baking sheet with aluminum foil, then spray evenly with cooking oil spray. Divide the chickpea batter evenly into 12 patties and arrange them on the baking sheet. Bake for 10 to 12 minutes, or until the patties are firm to the touch.

4. Serve the burgers on warmed sesame seed or kaiser rolls, with curly endive, red onion slices, and a spoonful of chutney.

The following analysis is based on 1 burger with bun and garnishes:

Calories: 356	Total fat: 7 g	Protein: 16 g
Carbohydrate: 54 g	Cholesterol: 36 g	Sodium: 259 mg

CREAMY COLESLAW

¼ cup reduced-fat mayonnaise or commercially
   prepared tofu mayonnaise
¾ cup plain, low-fat yogurt
4 ounces soft, low-fat cream cheese (Neufchâtel)
1-pound package pre-shredded coleslaw cabbage
   (preferably with carrots)
½ cup chopped fresh parsley
Salt and freshly ground pepper, to taste

1. In a small bowl, whisk together the mayonnaise, yogurt, and cream cheese.

2. Combine the coleslaw cabbage and parsley in a serving bowl. Pour the dressing over and toss to combine well, then season to taste with salt and pepper.

Calories: 122	Total fat: 8 g	Protein: 4 g
Carbohydrate: 9 g	Cholesterol: 22 g	Sodium: 177 mg

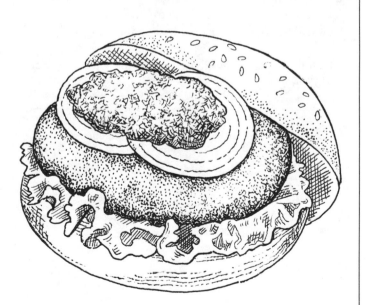

Pantry staples
❑ Madras or other good-quality curry
   powder
❑ Canola or olive oil
❑ Red onions, 2 medium
❑ Chickpeas, 2 1-pound cans

Refrigerator staples
❑ Reduced-fat mayonnaise or
   commercially prepared tofu
   mayonnaise
❑ Plain low-fat yogurt
❑ Egg, 1
❑ Toasted wheat germ

Shopping list: fresh foods and nonstaples
❑ Parsley, 1 bunch
❑ Walnuts, shelled
❑ Egg substitute or potato starch
   (if not using egg)
❑ Sesame-seed or kaiser rolls, 6 large
❑ Curly endive or other lettuce,
   1 head
❑ Prepared chutney, 1 small bottle
❑ Pre-shredded coleslaw cabbage,
   1-pound package
❑ Soft, low-fat cream cheese
   (Neufchâtel), portion of 8-ounce
   package

MENU

Pinto Bean Sloppy Joes

Zucchini-Broccoli Relish Salad

Microwaved potatoes or sweet potatoes

Serves 6

Here's a burger menu made even simpler by the fact that you need not even make, fry, and flip patties. Pinto beans stand in for the ground meat traditionally used in sloppy joes, but with a taste and texture all their own. This menu is likely to become a fixture in your repertoire if you have a penchant for simple, hearty meals.

Strategy:

1. Place potatoes or sweet potatoes in the microwave and bake, allowing the allotted amount of time per potato according to the wattage of your individual unit. If your unit is less than 750 watts, you might want to bake half of the potatoes at a time, serve everyone a half to start with while baking the remaining potatoes, and serve another half as a second helping. Otherwise, if baked together, they may not be done in the allotted time.

2. Prepare the Pinto Bean Sloppy Joes.

PINTO BEAN SLOPPY JOES

1 tablespoon olive oil
1 medium onion, finely chopped
½ medium green bell pepper, finely diced
1-pound can pinto or black beans, drained and rinsed
¼ cup wheat germ
1 cup thick tomato sauce or pureed tomatoes
1 tablespoon soy sauce
1 teaspoon honey or brown rice syrup
1 teaspoon chili powder
1 teaspoon paprika
½ teaspoon dried basil
6 whole-grain rolls

1. Heat the oil in a large, heavy saucepan. Add the onion and bell pepper and sauté for 3 to 4 minutes.

2. Add the remaining ingredients except the rolls and bring to a gentle simmer. With a potato masher, mash the beans until coarsely and evenly mashed. Simmer over medium-low heat, loosely covered, for 5 to 7 minutes, stirring occasionally. Serve at once on whole-grain rolls.

The following analysis is based on 1 sloppy joe sandwich, including a roll:

Calories: 263	Total fat: 4 g	Protein: 10 g
Carbohydrate: 46 g	Cholesterol: 0 g	Sodium: 427 mg

ZUCCHINI-BROCCOLI RELISH SALAD

2 medium zucchini, quartered lengthwise and diced
1 cup finely chopped broccoli florets
1 medium red bell pepper, cut into strips
¼ cup sweet pickle relish
½ cup reduced-fat mayonnaise or commercially
   prepared tofu mayonnaise

1. Combine all the ingredients in a serving bowl and stir
well to mix.

Calories: 89	Total fat: 5 g	Protein: 1 g
Carbohydrate: 9 g	Cholesterol: 7 g	Sodium: 204 mg

Strategy, continued

3. While the beans cook, prepare the
   Zucchini-Broccoli Relish Salad.

4. Assemble the sloppy joes and serve
   with the salad and baked potatoes.

Pantry staples
❑ Light olive oil
❑ Onion, 1 medium
❑ Pinto or black beans, 1-pound can
❑ Tomato sauce or tomato puree,
   8-ounce can, or portion of
   1-pound can
❑ Soy sauce
❑ Honey or brown rice syrup
❑ Chili powder
❑ Paprika
❑ Dried basil

Refrigerator staples
❑ Reduced-fat mayonnaise or
   commercially prepared tofu
   mayonnaise
❑ Toasted wheat germ

Shopping list: fresh foods and
   nonstaples
❑ Green bell pepper, 1 medium
❑ Red bell pepper, 1 medium
❑ Zucchini, 2 medium
❑ Broccoli, 1 small bunch or small
   quantity precut florets
❑ Sweet pickle relish, 1 small jar
❑ White or sweet potatoes, 1 per
   serving
❑ Whole-grain rolls, 6

MENU

White Bean Pâté

Crispbreads, crackers, and fresh breads

Olives and cherry tomatoes

Fresh fruit and cheese plate

Serves 4 to 6

Here's a simple yet sophisticated meal that's perfect for those times when you crave a light meal that doesn't involve much cooking. It makes a great late supper, served with wine, or a lovely lunch for company.

Strategy:

1. Prepare the pâté. While the onion and garlic mixture sautés, prepare small bowls of olives and cherry tomatoes; slice fresh bread and arrange it with crispbreads and crackers on a serving platter.

2. Process the pâté and transfer it to a crock.

3. Arrange a platter of fresh fruits according to season, and sliced cheeses. Include grapes, which are almost always available, with fresh pears or apples during cold-weather months, or melons and strawberries during summer months. Choose two varieties of cheese to serve. One of the

WHITE BEAN PÂTÉ

1 tablespoon canola oil
1 cup chopped onion
1 to 2 cloves garlic, minced
1-pound can white beans (great Northern or cannellini), drained and rinsed
Juice of ½ lemon
¼ cup parsley leaves
1 tablespoon soy sauce
¼ teaspoon dried thyme
¼ teaspoon dried basil
1 teaspoon ground cumin
Freshly ground pepper, to taste

1. Heat the oil in a skillet. Add the onion and garlic and sauté, covered, until golden, about 7 minutes, stirring occasionally.

2. Combine the onion-garlic mixture with the remaining ingredients in a food processor fitted with a steel blade. Process the bean mixture until smooth, then transfer it to a crock and pat it in.

| Calories: 102 | Total fat: 2 g | Protein: 5 g |
| Carbohydrate: 15 g | Cholesterol: 0 g | Sodium: 171 mg |

Strategy, continued

two cheeses should be semisoft (for spreading), such as a Neufchâtel cream cheese, creamy goat cheese, or Brie.

Pantry staples
- ❑ Onion, 1 large or 2 medium
- ❑ Canola oil
- ❑ White beans (great Northern or cannellini), 1-pound can
- ❑ Soy sauce
- ❑ Dried thyme
- ❑ Dried basil
- ❑ Ground cumin
- ❑ Black olives, 8-ounce or 1-pound can

Refrigerator staples
- ❑ Lemon, 1
- ❑ Fresh garlic

Shopping list: fresh foods and nonstaples
- ❑ Parsley, 1 small bunch
- ❑ Crispbreads and crackers
- ❑ Fresh bread of your choice
- ❑ Fresh fruit in season (grapes, plus apples and pears, or grapes, plus melons and strawberries)
- ❑ Cheese of choice, about 6 ounces
- ❑ Semisoft cheese of choice (Neufchâtel, goat cheese, or Brie), about 4 ounces
- ❑ Cherry tomatoes, 1 pint

——— MENU ———

Chunky Bean Spread

Refreshingly Fruited Red Cabbage Salad

Corn-on-the-cob

Serves 6

I live in the Northeast, where locally grown corn is a most anticipated crop in midsummer and early fall. However, fresh corn imported from other locales is available almost year-round, and I've been finding that this off-season corn seems to get better all the time. Fresh corn teamed with a hearty sandwich is my idea of a great, quick dinner prepared with little cooking and almost no fuss. The sandwich on its own makes a marvelous lunch.
— N. A.

Strategy:

1. Bring water to a boil in a large pot for the corn and cook it as needed. Or, if you prefer, you can microwave it in the allotted time if your unit is at least 750 watts.

2. Prepare the Refreshingly Fruited Red Cabbage Salad and set aside.

3. Prepare the Chunky Bean Spread. Serve all of these items together, and let everyone assemble their own sandwiches.

CHUNKY BEAN SPREAD

You can use leftovers of this tasty spread as a dip for tortilla chips. If using as a dip, thin the consistency with a bit of water if necessary.

½ medium green or red bell pepper, cut into 1-inch chunks
½ medium zucchini, cut into 1-inch chunks
⅓ cup pimiento-stuffed green olives
1 or 2 scallions, green part only, coarsely chopped
2 1-pound cans pinto beans, drained and rinsed
1 tablespoon lemon juice
½ teaspoon chili powder, or more to taste
½ teaspoon ground cumin, or more to taste
Fresh whole-grain or rye bread
Alfalfa sprouts
Dijon-style or spicy brown mustard (optional)
Reduced-fat mayonnaise or commercially prepared tofu mayonnaise (optional)

1. Combine the bell pepper, zucchini, olives, and scallions in the workbowl of a food processor fitted with a steel blade. Pulse the food processor on and off several times, until the pepper and zucchini are chopped into approximately ¼-inch pieces.

2. Add the beans, lemon juice, and seasonings, and pulse the food processor on and off until everything is evenly chopped, with a chunky texture.

3. Let everyone assemble their own sandwiches, spreading the bean mixture generously on one slice of bread, topping it with a handful of alfalfa sprouts, and covering it with another piece of bread that has been spread with mustard or mayonnaise, or left plain, as desired.

| Calories: 167 | Total fat: 1 g | Protein: 8 g |
| Carbohydrate: 31 g | Cholesterol: 0 g | Sodium: 106 mg |

REFRESHINGLY FRUITED RED CABBAGE SALAD

2 cups red cabbage, thinly shredded
1-pound can unsweetened crushed pineapple, drained
¼ cup raisins
1 tablespoon sesame seeds
1 teaspoon dark sesame oil
1 tablespoon honey or brown rice syrup
1 tablespoon lemon juice

1. Combine all the ingredients in a serving bowl and mix well. Cover and set aside until needed.

Calories: 89	Total fat: 2 g	Protein: 1 g
Carbohydrate: 18 g	Cholesterol: 0 g	Sodium: 6 mg

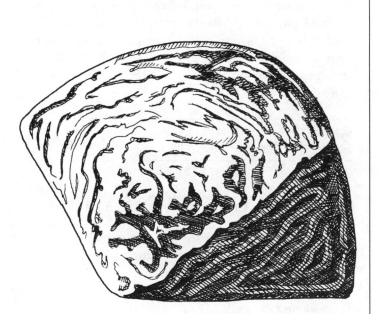

Pantry staples
- ❑ Pinto beans, 2 1-pound cans
- ❑ Chili powder
- ❑ Ground cumin
- ❑ Raisins
- ❑ Dark sesame oil
- ❑ Honey or brown rice syrup

Refrigerator staples
- ❑ Pimiento-stuffed green olives
- ❑ Lemon, 1
- ❑ Dijon-style or spicy brown mustard (optional)
- ❑ Reduced-fat mayonnaise or commercially prepared tofu mayonnaise (optional)

Shopping list: fresh foods and nonstaples
- ❑ Green or red bell pepper, 1 medium
- ❑ Zucchini, 1 medium
- ❑ Scallions, 1 bunch
- ❑ Red cabbage, 1 head
- ❑ Alfalfa sprouts
- ❑ Crushed pineapple, unsweetened, 1-pound can
- ❑ Fresh whole-grain or rye bread
- ❑ Sesame seeds, small quantity
- ❑ Corn-on-the-cob, 6 ears

MENU

Mozzarella in Carrozza

Cucumber Salad

Cool Tomato Cream Soup

Serves 6

Mozzarella in carrozza *is the Italian version of that perennial childhood favorite, the grilled cheese sandwich. The difference lies not just in the kind of bread and cheese used, but in the treatment as well. We've offset the richness of the dish with a cucumber salad and a bowl (or mug) of cool creamy tomato soup to make it a perfect warm-weather meal.*

Strategy:

1. Slice the cucumbers and mix them with the salad ingredients; cover and refrigerate until needed. Stir once or twice before serving time.

2. Assemble and grill the mozzarella sandwiches.

3. While grilling the first side of the sandwiches, prepare the recipe for Cool Tomato Cream Soup.

4. Grill the other side of the sandwiches.

MOZZARELLA IN CARROZZA

1 whole egg plus 2 egg whites, or ⅔ cup egg substitute
3 tablespoons low-fat milk
2 tablespoons soy margarine
6 large slices part-skim mozzarella cheese
12 slices Italian bread in ½-inch slices (use a loaf that is rounded rather than long and thin so you can get large slices from it)

1. Beat the eggs or egg substitute with the milk in a wide bowl.

2. Heat the margarine in a large, heavy skillet or on a griddle over moderate heat.

3. Make 6 sandwiches, using 1 slice of cheese and 2 slices of bread for each. When the margarine is hot, dip the sandwiches, one by one, into the egg mixture, then cook them in the skillet until golden brown on both sides. Serve at once with the tomato soup and the cucumber salad alongside.

Calories: 274	Total fat: 8 g	Protein: 14 g
Carbohydrate: 36 g	Cholesterol: 47 g	Sodium: 518 mg

CUCUMBER SALAD

3 medium cucumbers, peeled and thinly sliced
2 tablespoons honey, brown rice syrup, or sugar
2 tablespoons white-wine vinegar
2 tablespoons cold water
¼ teaspoon salt
1 tablespoon minced fresh dill or 1 teaspoon dried dill weed

1. Place the sliced cucumbers in a medium-sized serving bowl.

2. Combine the remaining ingredients in a small bowl and whisk together. Toss with the cucumbers, then refrigerate until needed, stirring once or twice until serving time.

Calories: 43	Total fat: 0 g	Protein: 1 g
Carbohydrate: 9 g	Cholesterol: 0 g	Sodium: 3 mg

COOL TOMATO CREAM SOUP

28- to 32-ounce can plum tomatoes packed in puree
    (see Note)
3 scallions, white and green, coarsely chopped
½ teaspoon honey, brown rice syrup, or sugar
Pinch of salt (optional)
1 cup low-fat sour cream or yogurt
¼ cup chopped fresh parsley, or more or less, to taste

1. Place all the ingredients except the parsley in a blender or food processor fitted with a steel blade and puree until smooth. Stir in the parsley.

2. Serve in small bowls that can be set on a plate and served alongside the cucumber salad and sandwiches.

Note: If you place the can of tomatoes in the refrigerator on the morning of the day you plan to make this, the soup will have a nicely chilled effect.

During tomato season, you may certainly substitute 2 pounds of fresh tomatoes. The soup will be smoother and better if you take the time to dunk the tomatoes into a pot of boiling water for a minute, then slip off the skins, but take into account that this will add a few more minutes to the prep time of the meal.

Calories: 54	Total fat: 1.5 g	Protein: 4 g
Carbohydrate: 8 g	Cholesterol: 3 g	Sodium: 42 mg

Pantry staples
❏ Honey, brown rice syrup, or granulated sugar
❏ White-wine vinegar
❏ Dried dill (use if fresh dill is unavailable)
❏ Plum tomatoes in puree, 28-ounce can

Refrigerator staples
❏ Eggs, 3, or egg substitute
❏ Low-fat milk
❏ Soy margarine

Shopping list: fresh foods and nonstaples
❏ Low-fat sour cream, 1-pint container, or plain, low-fat yogurt, 1 cup
❏ Cucumbers, 3 medium
❏ Italian bread, 1 loaf (rounded rather than long and narrow)
❏ Part-skim mozzarella cheese, 8-ounce package
❏ Scallions, 1 bunch
❏ Fresh parsley, 1 bunch
❏ Fresh dill, 1 bunch

MENU

Quick Pasta and Bean Soup

Vegetable Hero

Small seedless oranges

Serves 6

As a real soup aficionado, I find this an immensely satisfying meal. The pasta and bean soup is one that tastes as if it's been simmering for hours, and the vegetable-filled hero is a perfect counterpoint — hearty, but not heavy. Seedless oranges served at the end of the meal act as a nice palate refresher after all the robust and savory flavors.
— N. A.

Strategy:

1. Prepare the soup recipe through step 3.

2. Prepare the Vegetable Hero recipe.

3. Finish the last step of the soup recipe and serve it with the sandwiches. Pass around fresh oranges after the meal to refresh the palate.

QUICK PASTA AND BEAN SOUP

1 cup uncooked ditalini (tiny, tube-shaped pasta)
1 tablespoon olive oil
1 small zucchini, cut into ½-inch or smaller dice
2 cloves garlic, minced
2 1-pound cans cannellini (great Northern beans)
14-ounce can crushed or pureed tomatoes
2 teaspoons salt-free herb-and-spice seasoning blend
1 teaspoon paprika
½ teaspoon Italian herb seasoning blend,
    or more to taste
2 tablespoons finely chopped fresh parsley
Salt and freshly ground pepper, to taste

1. Bring water to a boil in a medium-sized saucepan. Cook the ditalini until *al dente,* then drain.

2. In the meantime, heat the oil in a soup pot. Add the zucchini and garlic and cook over moderate heat, covered, about 2 minutes.

3. Add the remaining ingredients except the parsley, along with 3 cups of water. Turn the heat up and bring the soup to a simmer, then turn the heat back to moderate and simmer the soup gently but steadily for 10 minutes, covered.

4. When the pasta is done, drain it and add it to the soup along with the parsley. Adjust the consistency with more water if the soup is too dense. Season to taste with salt and pepper, remove the soup from the heat, and serve.

Variation: Replace one of the cans of canellini with a can of chickpeas.

| Calories: 238 | Total fat: 3 g | Protein: 11 g |
| Carbohydrate: 41 g | Cholesterol: 0 g | Sodium: 296 mg |

VEGETABLE HERO

1 tablespoon olive oil
1 medium onion, quartered and thinly sliced
1 medium green or red bell pepper, cut into 2-inch
    strips
½ pound white mushrooms, wiped and thickly sliced
⅓ cup reduced-fat mayonnaise or commercially
    prepared tofu mayonnaise
1 teaspoon dried dill
Salt and freshly ground pepper, to taste
1 large loaf fresh Italian bread

1. Heat the olive oil in a large skillet. Add the onion, and over it layer the bell pepper, and over that the mushrooms. Cover the skillet tightly and cook the vegetables over moderate heat for 5 minutes, then remove from the heat.

2. Uncover and stir the vegetables. Add the mayonnaise and dill, season to taste with salt and pepper, then stir again.

3. Split the Italian bread in half horizontally, spread the flat bottom half with the filling, then cover with the top half. Cut into 6 equal segments and serve.

Calories: 294	Total fat: 5 g	Protein: 8 g
Carbohydrate: 41 g	Cholesterol: 4 g	Sodium: 527 mg

Pantry staples
❏ Olive oil
❏ Cannellini (great Northern beans),
    2 1-pound cans
❏ Crushed or pureed tomatoes,
    14-ounce can
❏ Onion, 1 medium
❏ Salt-free herb-and-spice seasoning
    blend
❏ Italian herb seasoning blend
❏ Paprika
❏ Dried dill

Refrigerator staples
❏ Reduced-fat mayonnaise or
    commercially prepared tofu
    mayonnaise
❏ Fresh garlic

*Shopping list: fresh foods and
    nonstaples*
❏ Ditalini (tiny, tubular pasta),
    1-pound box
❏ Zucchini, 1 small
❏ Fresh parsley, 1 small bunch
❏ Red or green bell pepper, 1
    medium
❏ Mushrooms, 8 ounces
❏ Fresh Italian bread, 1 large loaf
❏ Small seedless oranges, 6 to 8

MENU

Farmhouse Creamed Corn Soup

Black Olive Tapenade Pita Rolls

Roasted Asparagus with Sesame Seeds

Serves 6

Among the comfort foods from my past that I still enjoy is this corn soup. Since our school didn't have a lunch program, I went home for lunch each day, and this was one of the wonderful things my mother served us, along with hefty sandwiches and fresh fruit. These days my tastes are a bit more sophisticated, as in this menu with tapenade pita rolls as the companion dish. But I won't tamper with the soup; it remains exactly the way my mother used to make it. A simple roast of fresh asparagus adds just the right touch of green. When asparagus is not in season, substitute any steamed green vegetable of your choice.
— L. K.

Strategy:

1. Preheat the oven or toaster oven to 425 degrees.

2. Combine all the ingredients for the creamed corn soup in a heavy saucepan, cover, and set over low heat.

3. Stack the pita breads, wrap them in foil, and place them in the oven or toaster oven for 5 minutes.

FARMHOUSE CREAMED CORN SOUP

2 1-pound cans creamed corn
12-ounce can evaporated skim milk
2½ cups low-fat or skim milk
¼ teaspoon salt
2 tablespoons honey, brown rice syrup, or sugar, or to taste

1. Combine all the ingredients in a soup pot. Heat slowly, stirring occasionally, until hot. Do not allow to boil. Cover and let stand off the heat until needed.

Calories: 224	Total fat: 2 g	Protein: 10 g
Carbohydrate: 41 g	Cholesterol: 7 g	Sodium: 128 mg

BLACK OLIVE TAPENADE PITA ROLLS

½ cup pitted black olives (any size)
4-ounce jar Greek olives, pitted and drained
½ cup capers, drained (or substitute ½ cup pimiento-stuffed green olives)
2 cloves garlic, minced
½ teaspoon dried thyme
1 rounded tablespoon Dijon-style mustard
Lemon juice, to taste
Freshly ground pepper, to taste
3 large (10-inch diameter) or 6 regular-sized fresh pita breads, split in half to make 6 or 12 rounds, warmed
Alfalfa sprouts
Sliced tomatoes for garnish

1. In a food processor fitted with a steel blade, finely chop the olives. Add the capers, garlic, thyme, and mustard; puree. Add the lemon juice and pepper to taste.

2. Lay the warmed pita bread halves, baked side down, on a work surface. Divide the tapenade among them, spreading it with a spatula to cover the entire surface, but stopping within the last 2 inches of the far end. Scatter the sprouts over the tapenade, and then roll up tightly as if for a jelly roll. Place the tapenade rolls on each serving plate seam side down.

3. Serve the rolls whole to eat like a burrito or slice them in halves or thirds. Garnish with slices of ripe tomato.

Calories: 219	Total fat: 9 g	Protein: 6 g
Carbohydrate: 30 g	Cholesterol: 0 g	Sodium: 721 mg

ROASTED ASPARAGUS WITH SESAME SEEDS

The high heat brings to the surface all the sweet fresh flavor of this springtime delight. Serve it hot from the oven or at room temperature. Either way, it's a treat.

1½ pounds fresh asparagus, trimmed of tough woody ends
Olive oil cooking spray
3 tablespoons untoasted sesame seeds

1. Preheat the oven or toaster oven to 425 degrees.

2. Lightly and evenly spray the asparagus spears with the olive oil spray.

3. Spread the spears out in a single layer in a shallow heavy pan and sprinkle with the sesame seeds. Roast, uncovered, for about 8 to 10 minutes, or until the spears are just tender when pierced with the tip of a knife. Watch them carefully so that they don't overbake! Remove them from the oven, arrange on a platter, and serve.

Calories: 59	Total fat: 2 g	Protein: 3 g
Carbohydrate: 6 g	Cholesterol: 0 g	Sodium: 6 mg

Strategy, continued

4. Arrange the asparagus spears on a baking tray, and bake 10 minutes.

5. Prepare the recipe for Black Olive Tapenade Pita Rolls.

Pantry staples
- ❏ Olive oil cooking spray
- ❏ Dried thyme
- ❏ Black olives, pitted, 8-ounce can, or portion of 1-pound can

Refrigerator staples
- ❏ Fresh garlic
- ❏ Low-fat or skim milk, 3 cups
- ❏ Lemon, 1
- ❏ Dijon-style mustard

Shopping list: fresh foods and nonstaples
- ❏ Cream-style corn, 2 15-ounce or 1-pound cans
- ❏ Evaporated skim milk, 1 12-ounce can
- ❏ Asparagus, 1½ pounds
- ❏ Greek olives, pitted, 1 4-ounce jar
- ❏ Capers, 1 small jar (or substitute pimiento-stuffed green olives)
- ❏ Alfalfa sprouts
- ❏ Pita breads, 3 large (10-inch diameter) or 6 regular-sized
- ❏ Tomatoes, 2 or 3 medium
- ❏ Sesame seeds, untoasted, small quantity

MENU

Eggless "Egg Salad" Pitas

Mushroom Broth with Rice and Snow Peas

Half-sour dill pickle spears and tomato wedges

Serves 4

Tofu is a culinary chameleon, taking on many forms, depending on what it's surrounded by and flavored with. Here, it takes on the form of egg salad, which, when made with eggs and regular mayonnaise, is a high-fat, high-cholesterol combination that many of us prefer to avoid. But this mock egg salad, made with tofu and tofu mayonnaise and teamed with pickles, tomatoes, and a soothing broth, is a treat that won't rub you and your healthy eating habits the wrong way.

Strategy:

1. Begin preparing the soup.

2. During the simmering intervals, prepare the "egg salad."

3. Warm the pitas and cut the pickles and tomatoes.

4. The soup can be served first, or along with the pita sandwiches.

EGGLESS "EGG SALAD" PITAS

1 pound medium-firm tofu, drained
1 large stalk celery, finely diced
1 scallion, finely chopped
⅓ cup commercially prepared tofu mayonnaise
1 to 2 teaspoons Dijon-style mustard, to taste
1 teaspoon good-quality curry powder
Salt and freshly ground pepper, to taste
4 pita breads, warmed
Alfalfa sprouts or shredded lettuce (optional)

1. Break the tofu into several pieces, place it in a mixing bowl, and finely crumble it with a fork. Add the diced celery and scallion.

2. In a small bowl, combine the mayonnaise, mustard, and curry powder and mix well. Pour the mayonnaise mixture over the tofu mixture, stir well, and season to taste with salt and pepper.

3. Cut each pita bread in half and let everyone stuff their own pitas with the tofu mixture, along with some alfalfa sprouts or shredded lettuce if desired. Serve with dill pickle spears and tomato wedges.

| Calories: 286 | Total fat: 11 g | Protein: 14 g |
| Carbohydrate: 32 g | Cholesterol: 0 g | Sodium: 532 mg |

MUSHROOM BROTH WITH RICE AND SNOW PEAS

1-pound can vegetable broth
2 cups sliced small white mushrooms
1 cup snow peas, trimmed and cut in half
2 scallions, sliced
1 cup raw quick-cooking brown rice
1 tablespoon soy sauce
Freshly ground pepper, to taste

1. Combine the broth with 2 cups of water in a large saucepan and bring it to a boil.

2. While the liquid is coming to a boil, slice the mushrooms; prepare the snow peas and scallions. When the liquid comes to a boil, add the mushrooms and rice; lower the heat to moderate and simmer for 5 minutes.

3. Add the snow peas, scallions, and soy sauce. Simmer for 5 minutes more, season to taste with pepper, and serve.

Calories: 135	Total fat: 0 g	Protein: 4 g
Carbohydrate: 27 g	Cholesterol: 0 g	Sodium: 257 mg

Pantry staples
❑ Quick-cooking brown rice
❑ Soy sauce
❑ Curry powder

Refrigerator staples
❑ Dijon-style mustard
❑ Celery, 1 stalk

Shopping list: fresh foods and nonstaples
❑ Vegetable broth, 1-pound can
❑ Small white mushrooms, about 8 ounces
❑ Snow peas, about 4 ounces
❑ Scallions, 1 bunch
❑ Tofu, medium-firm, 1 pound
❑ Tofu mayonnaise, 1 jar
❑ Half-sour dill pickles, as desired
❑ Tomatoes, 2 to 3 medium
❑ Alfalfa sprouts, or lettuce, any variety (optional)
❑ Pita breads, package of 6

MENU

Vegetable Rarebit

Greens with Oranges and Sweet Vinaigrette

Steamed broccoli

Serves 4

Rarebit is a classic Welsh dish featuring a rich cheese sauce traditionally served over toast. This version features small vegetable bits and reduced-fat cheddar cheese, to help stretch the volume and cut the fat content at the same time. The salad with sweet vinaigrette is one I've enjoyed at a friend's home several times; it's simple, with a harmony of light flavors that makes it compatible with many types of hearty dishes.
— *N. A.*

Strategy:

1. Prepare the sweet vinaigrette and set aside.

2. Prepare the Vegetable Rarebit.

3. Prepare the salad.

4. Combine the florets from about 2 medium bunches of broccoli, or about 1 pound of precut fresh broccoli florets, with about an inch of water in a deep heavy saucepan and steam until tender-crisp.

VEGETABLE RAREBIT

1 small zucchini, quartered and sliced
2 cups sliced white mushrooms
1 cup diced fresh tomato
1 cup frozen peas, thawed
2 tablespoons unbleached white flour
8 ounces pre-grated reduced-fat cheddar cheese (see Note)
½ cup beer
1 teaspoon dry mustard
Dash of cayenne pepper
8 slices whole-grain bread

1. Combine the first 4 ingredients in a large, heavy saucepan with about an inch of water. Cover and steam over moderate heat for 4 to 5 minutes, or until all are lightly cooked.

2. Sprinkle in the flour and stir until well blended, then sprinkle in the cheese, about half at a time, and melt slowly, stirring.

3. Once the cheese is smoothly melted, slowly stir in the beer, pouring in a little at a time. Stir in the spices and cook over very low heat for another 2 minutes.

4. In the meantime, toast 8 slices of whole-grain bread. Arrange 2 slices on each plate, then distribute the cheese sauce over them and serve at once, open-faced.

Note: While reduced-fat cheddar works well in this dish, nonfat cheddar doesn't.

Calories: 267	Total fat: 11 g	Protein: 20 g
Carbohydrate: 17 g	Cholesterol: 41 g	Sodium: 416 mg

GREENS WITH ORANGES AND SWEET VINAIGRETTE

Sweet vinaigrette
⅓ cup olive oil
⅓ cup red-wine vinegar
3 tablespoons granulated sugar

Dark green lettuce leaves, torn, as desired
2 small seedless oranges such as Clementines or sweet
    Mineolas, peeled and sectioned
Red onion slices, as desired
¼ cup toasted slivered almonds

1. Combine the ingredients for the sweet vinaigrette in a tightly lidded cruet and shake well. Set aside until needed.

2. In a salad bowl, toss the lettuce with the orange sections. Scatter some red onion slices over the top, followed by the slivered almonds.

3. Serve in individual salad bowls. Pass around the vinaigrette, letting everyone dress their own salad as they wish. Shake well before each use.

The following analysis is based on using 1 tablespoon of dressing per serving:

Calories: 171	Total fat: 11 g	Protein: 2 g
Carbohydrate: 15 g	Cholesterol: 0 g	Sodium: 3 mg

Strategy, continued

5. Toast the bread for the rarebit.

6. Serve the rarebit and broccoli together on a plate; serve the salad in bowls on the side, and pass the vinaigrette around so that everyone can dress their own salad.

Pantry staples
❑ Olive oil
❑ Red-wine vinegar
❑ Granulated sugar
❑ Dry mustard
❑ Cayenne pepper
❑ Red onion, approximately 1 medium
❑ Unbleached white flour

Freezer staples
❑ Green peas, portion of 10-ounce box or 1-pound bag

Shopping list: fresh foods and nonstaples
❑ Zucchini, 1 small
❑ White mushrooms, about ½ pound
❑ Tomatoes, about 2 medium
❑ Grated reduced-fat cheddar cheese, 8-ounce package
❑ Beer, 1 can or small bottle
❑ Dark green lettuce, such as romaine or other, 1 head
❑ Small seedless oranges such as Clementines or sweet Mineolas, 2
❑ Toasted slivered almonds, 1 small package

MENU

Gazpacho

Dilled Tofu Spread

Dark rye or pumpernickel bread, or fresh bagels

Serves 4 to 6

No wonder gazpacho is such a summer classic — this spicy, cold Spanish soup of raw vegetables needs no cooking at all. Teamed with a dill-scented tofu spread, it's a light, satisfying meal that's great for the hottest of days because you won't need to turn on a single burner. For those who think they don't like tofu, we predict that the first bite of the delectable spread will change your mind.

Strategy:

1. Prepare the gazpacho.

2. Prepare the Dilled Tofu Spread.

3. Slice the bread or bagels and arrange on a platter.

GAZPACHO

Under less rushed circumstances, you would want to chill the gazpacho for an hour or two before serving it. It is certainly still delicious eaten shortly after it is made, but for a cooler effect, you might want to refrigerate the canned plum tomatoes and tomato juice on the morning of the day you plan to make it.

Base
1 pound very ripe, juicy tomatoes, cut into chunks
⅔ large cucumber, peeled and cut into chunks
⅔ large green or red bell pepper, cut into chunks
2 scallions, coarsely chopped
A handful of parsley sprigs

To finish the soup
3 cups tomato juice, or as needed
⅓ large cucumber, peeled and finely diced
⅓ large green or red bell pepper, finely diced
2 fresh plum tomatoes, finely diced
1 medium celery stalk, finely diced
Juice of ½ to 1 lemon, to taste
2 teaspoons chili powder, or to taste
Salt and freshly ground pepper, to taste

1. Place all of the ingredients for the soup base in a food processor fitted with a steel blade. Puree until fairly smooth.

2. Stir in just enough tomato juice to give the soup a slightly thick consistency, then add the remaining ingredients. Stir together, and refrigerate the soup while preparing the rest of the meal.

Calories: 70	Total fat: 0 g	Protein: 2 g
Carbohydrate: 15 g	Cholesterol: 0 g	Sodium: 28 mg

DILLED TOFU SPREAD

8 ounces firm tofu
1 tablespoon white-wine vinegar or lemon juice
1 tablespoon soy sauce
2 scallions, finely chopped
1 stalk celery, finely chopped
2 to 3 tablespoons pickle relish, drained, or to taste
1 tablespoon minced fresh dill, or 1 teaspoon dried dill

1. Drain the tofu well and break it into several pieces. Place the tofu, vinegar, and soy sauce in a food processor fitted with a steel blade. Process until completely smooth.

2. Transfer the tofu mixture to a bowl and stir in the scallions, celery, relish, and dill. Serve as a spread with fresh rye or pumpernickel bread, or fresh bagels.

Calories: 47	Total fat: 2 g	Protein: 4 g
Carbohydrate: 4 g	Cholesterol: 0 g	Sodium: 254 mg

Pantry staples
❑ White-wine vinegar (if not using lemon juice)
❑ Soy sauce
❑ Chili powder
❑ Dried dill (if not using fresh)

Refrigerator staples
❑ Celery
❑ Pickle relish
❑ Lemon, 1

Shopping list: fresh foods and nonstaples
❑ Firm tofu, 8 ounces
❑ Scallions, 1 bunch
❑ Cucumber, 1 large
❑ Green or red bell pepper, 1 large
❑ Ripe, juicy tomatoes, 1 pound
❑ Plum tomatoes, 2
❑ Parsley, 1 bunch
❑ Fresh dill, 1 small bunch
❑ Tomato juice, 32-ounce can or bottle
❑ Fresh dark rye or pumpernickel bread, or fresh bagels

Chapter Five

NO MORE
MEAT-CRAVING BLUES

W e know many people who have given up meat, or almost have; but still, from time to time, they experience the craving for some familiar meat dish, with all the memories inherent in its flavors, textures, and aromas. Then there are others who feel they really should cut back on meat consumption for health reasons, but find it difficult for similar reasons — habits just die hard.

With these dilemmas in mind, we thought it would be fun to present this brief chapter of menus based on today's healthful meat analogs, most of which are readily available at any natural food store. This set of menus is intended as an introduction to these products and to demonstrate how they can be used easily and quickly. For those of you changing to more meatless meals, these menus may ease the transition when those cravings set in. For those of you already settled into a vegetarian way of life, these menus can be a pleasant way to re-create memorable meals from your past, minus the fat, cholesterol — and guilt!

Finally, if you belong to a family or group in which some say no to meat while others just won't give it up, these menus can serve as a common ground and please even those dyed-in-the-wool carnivores. And if Dad (or whoever) doesn't notice that the textured stuff in his chili is soy and not beef, don't worry — your secret is certainly safe with us!

Seitan Stroganoff
Wide Noodles with Poppy Seeds
Steamed fresh sugar snap peas (in season) or green beans
Simple tossed salad

Salisbury Seitan "Steak"
Wild Rice Salad with Pecans
Sliced tomatoes

Curried "Chicken" Salad
Sweet Tomato-Orange Salad
Pita or multigrain bread
Microwaved potatoes (optional)

"Filet" of Tofu with Mustard-Dill Sauce
Quick Brown Rice Salad with Raisins, Fennel, and Nuts

"Chicken" Chow Mein
Spinach-Citrus Salad

Easy TVP Chili
Tossed salad
Quick-cooking brown rice, couscous, or quinoa
Steamed green vegetable (broccoli, asparagus, or string beans)

TVP Sloppy Joes
Summer Squash and Corn Sauté
Half-sour dill pickles
Fat-free tortilla chips

Southern Ranch-Style Beans with "Frankfurters"
Steamed broccoli
Simple coleslaw
Fresh rye bread

MENU

Seitan Stroganoff

Wide Noodles with Poppy Seeds

Steamed fresh sugar snap peas (in season) or green beans

Simple tossed salad

Serves 6

Time was not so long ago when good thick sour cream was the secret to a successful Stroganoff. That hasn't changed, but sour cream certainly has. Available now in low-fat and even fat-free versions, it happily works in a way not yet achieved by low-fat cheese. Just remember that whichever you choose, the same rules apply. Don't let the sauce come to a boil or it will curdle.

Strategy:

1. Start cooking the egg noodles.

2. Prepare the Stroganoff through step 1.

3. Steam about a pound of sugar snap peas or green beans.

4. Prepare a simple tossed salad.

5. Finish cooking the Stroganoff.

6. Add a dressing to the salad.

SEITAN STROGANOFF

Seitan is the Japanese name for cooked wheat gluten, a remarkable, high-protein product prevalent in both Japanese and Chinese cookery. In vegetarian cookery, it is commonly used as an analog for beef. Seitan is widely available in natural food stores.

1 tablespoon canola oil
1 medium onion, sliced lengthwise into thin wedges
1 pound mushrooms, quartered
2 cloves garlic, minced
1 pound fresh seitan, sliced into thin julienne-style pieces
Salt, to taste
1 heaping tablespoon tomato paste
1 cup low-fat sour cream
1 tablespoon cornstarch

1. Heat the oil in a large, heavy skillet. Sauté the onion over medium heat until translucent, about 3 to 4 minutes, stirring occasionally. Add the mushrooms and garlic, raise the heat slightly, and sauté for 5 minutes more, covered, stirring occasionally, or until the onion is tender and the mushrooms are slightly wilted.

2. Stir in the seitan and cook for 10 minutes longer, stirring occasionally. Add 1 cup of water, salt, and the tomato paste. Bring to a simmer and remove from the heat.

3. In a small bowl, blend the sour cream and cornstarch until smooth. Off the heat, stir the sour cream mixture into the seitan mixture, return it to low heat, and simmer gently for 2 minutes only, or until thickened. Do not allow it to boil! Serve over the Wide Noodles with Poppy Seeds.

Helpful tip: Freeze leftover tomato paste in tablespoon-sized portions in ice cube tray compartments, and store the cubes in a plastic bag or container.

Calories: 232	Total fat: 7 g	Protein: 28 g
Carbohydrate: 12 g	Cholesterol: 3 g	Sodium: 24 mg

WIDE NOODLES WITH POPPY SEEDS

12-ounce package wide, yolk-free egg noodles
1½ to 2 tablespoons butter or soy margarine
1½ tablespoons poppy seeds
Salt and freshly ground pepper, to taste

1. Bring water to a boil in a large pot, and cook the noodles according to package directions until just tender. Drain the noodles over a bowl so that you can reserve 1 cup of the hot cooking water.

2. Return the noodles to the cooking pot, add the butter or margarine, reserved water, poppy seeds, salt and freshly ground pepper, and toss well. Cover until needed.

Calories: 109	Total fat: 4 g	Protein: 2 g
Carbohydrate: 14 g	Cholesterol: 26 g	Sodium: 2 mg

Pantry staples
- ❏ Canola oil
- ❏ Tomato paste
- ❏ Cornstarch
- ❏ Poppy seeds
- ❏ Onion, 1 medium

Refrigerator staples
- ❏ Reduced-fat sour cream
- ❏ Fresh garlic
- ❏ Butter or soy margarine

Shopping list: fresh foods and nonstaples
- ❏ Seitan, 1 pound fresh or frozen
- ❏ White mushrooms, 1 pound
- ❏ Wide yolk-free egg noodles, 12-ounce package
- ❏ Sugar snap peas (in season) or green beans, about 1 pound
- ❏ Salad vegetables of choice

MENU

Salisbury Seitan "Steak"

Wild Rice Salad with Pecans

Sliced tomatoes

Serves 4

You don't have to give up chewing satisfaction just because you've given up meat. Seitan, or cooked wheat gluten, provides all the chewy satisfaction your jaws could crave, especially when prepared like cutlets. Bring the whole meal together in a contemporary way by serving it with a "wild" salad of rice and pecans.

Strategy:

1. Cook the quick-cooking wild rice for the Wild Rice Salad, according to package directions. Set aside to cool.

2. Prepare the Salisbury Seitan "Steaks."

3. Complete the Wild Rice Salad.

4. Slice tomatoes and drizzle them with dressing, if desired.

SALISBURY SEITAN "STEAK"

1 pound fresh seitan, cut into ¼-inch-thick slices
Dijon mustard
Cornmeal
2 tablespoons canola oil
1 small onion, chopped
2 cloves garlic, minced
3 tablespoons unbleached white flour
2 to 3 tablespoons soy sauce, to taste

1. Lightly brush both sides of the seitan "steaks" with the mustard. Dip each into cornmeal to coat well on both sides.

2. Heat the oil in a large, nonstick skillet. When the oil is hot, reduce the heat to medium, add the "steaks," and brown first one side, then turn and brown the other. Remove them and place in a covered container to keep warm.

3. Sauté the onion and garlic in the same skillet for 3 to 4 minutes, stirring, until tender.

4. Sprinkle the flour into the onion-garlic mixture and cook slowly, stirring, until smooth. Add the soy sauce and 1½ cups of water, stir, and bring to a simmer. Cook gently until smooth and thickened. Add seitan "steaks" and reheat gently over very low heat for 2 minutes.

Calories: 281	Total fat: 7 g	Protein: 16 g
Carbohydrate: 20 g	Cholesterol: 0 g	Sodium: 599 mg

WILD RICE SALAD WITH PECANS

2¾-ounce package quick-cooking wild rice
1⅓ cups vegetable broth (canned or made from granules and water)
½ cup chopped pecans
1 cup frozen green peas, thoroughly thawed
1 large carrot, shredded in food processor or diced by hand
1 large celery stalk, diced

Dressing
2 tablespoons canola oil
2 tablespoons red-wine vinegar
1 tablespoon Dijon mustard
Salt and freshly ground pepper, to taste

1. Cook the wild rice following package directions, using the vegetable broth instead of water and omitting the butter or margarine that is usually recommended. When the rice is done, transfer it into a large bowl and fluff it with a fork. Allow it to cool to room temperature.

2. When the rice is cooled, add the pecans, peas, carrot, and celery, and toss.

3. In a small bowl, whisk together the dressing ingredients, then toss it well with the wild rice mixture.

Calories: 176	Total fat: 13 g	Protein: 3 g
Carbohydrate: 12 g	Cholesterol: 0 g	Sodium: 123 mg

Pantry staples
❏ Canola oil
❏ Red-wine vinegar
❏ Cornmeal
❏ Unbleached white flour
❏ Regular or low-sodium soy sauce
❏ Onion, 1 small

Refrigerator staples
❏ Dijon-style mustard
❏ Carrot, 1 large
❏ Celery, 1 large stalk
❏ Fresh garlic

Freezer staples
❏ Frozen green peas, portion of 10-ounce package or 1-pound bag

Shopping list: fresh foods and nonstaples
❏ Seitan, 1 pound fresh
❏ Quick-cooking wild rice, 2¾-ounce package
❏ Vegetable broth, 1-pound can
❏ Shelled pecans, small quantity
❏ Ripe tomatoes, 2 or 3 medium

MENU

Curried "Chicken" Salad

Sweet Tomato-Orange Salad

Pita or multigrain bread

Microwaved potatoes (optional)

Serves 4 to 6

You might not be able to tell the difference between this "chicken" salad and the real thing. Made with tofu and a vegetable-based flavoring, all it needs is a few raisins, walnuts, and a creamy curry sauce to fool the eye and the palate. As for the side salad, did you know that the tomato is not a vegetable at all (botanically speaking) but, like oranges, a fruit? That makes it a perfect flavor team with which to complement the spicy salad. This makes a delightfully different lunch or a light yet satisfying dinner.

Strategy:

1. If you're serving this meal with potatoes, place one potato per serving in the microwave, set time, and bake. Your unit should be at least 750 watts for them to be done in the allotted time. Otherwise, bake only 2 or 3 potatoes at a time, serve half to each person, then bake the rest to serve as second helpings.

CURRIED "CHICKEN" SALAD

1 pound extra-firm tofu
⅓ cup walnuts, finely chopped
⅔ cup golden seedless raisins
2 teaspoons vegetable-based "chicken" flavoring (see Note)
1 tablespoon lemon juice
½ cup plain, low-fat yogurt
¼ cup reduced-fat mayonnaise or commercially prepared tofu mayonnaise
2 teaspoons curry powder, preferably Madras or other good-quality, or to taste
Salt and freshly ground pepper, to taste
Pita or multigrain bread
Lettuce leaves

1. Cut the tofu into ¼-inch-thick slices. Blot the slices between paper towels or clean tea towels to remove excess water. Then, cut the slices into small dice and combine them in a large bowl with the walnuts and raisins.

2. In a small bowl or measuring cup, combine the chicken flavoring, lemon juice, yogurt, mayonnaise, curry powder, and salt and pepper. Stir this mixture into the tofu mixture. Serve in pita pockets with lettuce, or as a salad on lettuce-lined plates, accompanied by multigrain bread.

Note: Vegetable-based "chicken" flavoring is available in natural food stores. If you can't find it, you can substitute an equal amount of poultry seasoning, which is available in the spice section of supermarkets. Both are, in spite of their names, vegetarian products.

| Calories: 227 | Total fat: 12 g | Protein: 9 g |
| Carbohydrate: 21 g | Cholesterol: 6 g | Sodium: 107 mg |

SWEET TOMATO-ORANGE SALAD

Lettuce leaves, preferably Boston or Bibb
3 large ripe firm tomatoes, cored
3 navel or Temple oranges, peeled
Prepared Catalina or Pennsylvania Dutch–style sweet-
    and-sour salad dressing

1. Line one large or 4 individual salad plates with lettuce;
set aside.

2. With a long, sharp slicing knife, slice the tomatoes and
oranges horizontally into ¼-inch-thick slices. Arrange al-
ternating slices on top of the lettuce. Drizzle with dressing and serve at once.

Calories: 70	Total fat: 0 g	Protein: 2 g
Carbohydrate: 15 g	Cholesterol: 0 g	Sodium: 12 mg

Strategy, continued

2. Prepare the Curried "Chicken" Salad.

3. Prepare the tomato-orange salad.

Pantry staples
❑ Curry powder, preferably Madras, or other good-quality

Refrigerator staples
❑ Plain yogurt
❑ Mayonnaise, reduced-fat, or commercially prepared tofu mayonnaise
❑ Lemon, 1

Shopping list: fresh foods and nonstaples
❑ Extra-firm tofu, 1 pound
❑ Vegetable-based "chicken" flavoring (or substitute poultry seasoning)
❑ Walnuts, shelled, small quantity
❑ Golden seedless raisins, 1 box
❑ Boston or Bibb lettuce, 1 medium head
❑ Ripe tomatoes, 3 large
❑ Navel or Temple oranges, 3 large
❑ Catalina or Pennsylvania Dutch–style sweet-and-sour salad dressing
❑ Pita breads, 6, or multigrain bread, 1 loaf

MENU

"Filet" of Tofu with Mustard-Dill Sauce

Quick Brown Rice Salad with Raisins, Fennel, and Nuts

Serves 4

Usually served with an herb-cured salmon, this traditional Scandinavian sauce works every bit as well with tofu. A quick sauté in a skillet and it's ready for the table, complemented by a sturdy rice salad sparked with crunchy fennel, raisins, and nuts.

Strategy:

1. Do steps 1 and 2 of the tofu recipe.

2. While the tofu is sautéing, prepare the rice salad.

3. Complete the tofu recipe.

"FILET" OF TOFU WITH MUSTARD-DILL SAUCE

1-pound package extra-firm tofu, cut into ¼-inch-thick slices
1 tablespoon canola oil

Sauce
¼ cup dark grainy mustard
1 teaspoon dry mustard
1 tablespoon honey or brown rice syrup
2 tablespoons white-wine vinegar
2 tablespoons reduced-fat mayonnaise, or commercially prepared tofu mayonnaise
3 tablespoons fresh chopped dill, or 1 tablespoon dried dill

Garnish
4 Roma or plum tomatoes
Parsley sprigs

1. Blot the tofu slices between paper towels or clean tea towels briefly to remove excess moisture.

2. Heat the oil in a large, nonstick skillet, and sauté the tofu until pale gold on both sides.

3. Combine all the ingredients for the sauce in a small bowl and stir well.

4. When the tofu is done, drain it on paper towels, and arrange it in rows on a serving plate. Spoon the mustard-dill dressing over the tofu slices.

5. Garnish with tomatoes thinly sliced almost, but not quite, through to the stem end. Fan each tomato out, arrange on a plate with the tofu slices, and garnish with a few sprigs of fresh parsley.

Calories: 181	Total fat: 13 g	Protein: 8 g
Carbohydrate: 8 g	Cholesterol: 3 g	Sodium: 476 mg

QUICK BROWN RICE SALAD WITH RAISINS, FENNEL, AND NUTS

2 cups raw quick brown rice
1-pound can vegetable broth
2 tablespoons canola oil
2 tablespoons lemon juice
1 teaspoon finely minced fresh ginger, or ¼ teaspoon ground ginger
Salt and freshly ground black pepper, to taste
1 small fennel bulb, trimmed, quartered, cored, and thinly sliced
½ cup dark raisins
⅓ to ½ cup coarsely chopped walnuts

1. Following package directions, prepare the rice, using the vegetable broth instead of water. When it's done, fluff it with a fork, transfer it to a large bowl, and allow it to cool while preparing the remaining ingredients.

2. In a small bowl, whisk together the oil, lemon juice, and ginger. Toss with the rice. Season to taste with salt and pepper. Add the fennel, raisins, and walnuts and toss again. Serve at room temperature.

Calories: 337	Total fat: 12 g	Protein: 6 g
Carbohydrate: 59 g	Cholesterol: 0 g	Sodium: 20 mg

Pantry staples
❏ Canola oil
❏ Dark grainy mustard
❏ Dry mustard
❏ Dried dill (unless using fresh)
❏ Honey or brown rice syrup
❏ White-wine vinegar
❏ Dark raisins
❏ Quick-cooking brown rice
❏ Ground ginger (if not using fresh)

Refrigerator staples
❏ Lemon, 1
❏ Reduced-fat mayonnaise or commercially prepared tofu mayonnaise

Shopping list: fresh foods and nonstaples
❏ Extra-firm water-packed tofu, 1 pound
❏ Vegetable broth, 1-pound can
❏ Ginger, fresh
❏ Fennel, 1 small bulb
❏ Walnuts, 1 small package
❏ Dill, 1 small bunch
❏ Roma or plum tomatoes, 4
❏ Parsley, 1 bunch

MENU

"Chicken" Chow Mein

Spinach-Citrus Salad

Serves 6

Baked pressed tofu is becoming a staple in natural food stores. It is savory and chewy, and will surprise anyone who thinks they don't like tofu because it is bland and mushy. In fact, in a mélange-style dish such as this chow mein, it might fool anyone who isn't told that it is tofu.

Strategy:

1. Cook the rice for the "Chicken" Chow Mein.

2. Continue with the chow mein recipe, and make the spinach salad and its dressing during odd moments of its preparation.

"CHICKEN" CHOW MEIN

6-serving portion quick-cooking brown rice
1 tablespoon canola oil
2 teaspoons dark sesame oil
1 large onion, quartered and thinly sliced
2 large celery stalks, sliced diagonally
1 large red bell pepper, diced
1 to 1½ cups sliced white mushrooms
8-ounce package fresh mung bean sprouts
1 tablespoon cornstarch
½ cup canned vegetable stock or water
2 tablespoons soy sauce, or to taste
8-ounce package baked pressed tofu, cut into
    thin strips
2 scallions, sliced diagonally
½ cup toasted unsalted cashews

1. Cook the rice according to package directions. When it's done, fluff it with a fork and cover; let it stand off the heat until needed.

2. Heat the oils in a very large skillet or wok. Add the onion and celery and sauté over medium-high heat, covered, for 4 to 5 minutes, stirring occasionally.

3. Layer the bell pepper, mushrooms, and sprouts over the onion-celery mixture. Cover and cook for about 5 minutes, or until the sprouts are slightly wilted, then stir all the vegetables together.

4. Dissolve the cornstarch in the stock or water, then stir in the soy sauce. Pour the cornstarch mixture over the vegetables in the skillet or wok, followed by the tofu and scallions. Cook for 5 minutes more over moderate heat, until the sauce has thickened up.

5. Scatter the cashews over the top and serve the chow mein from the skillet or wok, placing each serving over a bed of rice.

Calories: 326	Total fat: 12 g	Protein: 10 g
Carbohydrate: 45 g	Cholesterol: 0 g	Sodium: 357 mg

SPINACH-CITRUS SALAD

5 to 6 ounces (half of a 10- or 12-ounce package) fresh "triple-washed" spinach, rinsed
1 large cucumber, quartered and seeded, then cut into 2-inch lengths (peel only if waxed)
2 cups coarsely shredded red cabbage
1 to 2 small seedless oranges, such as Clementines or tangelos, peeled and sectioned

Dressing
2 tablespoons undiluted orange juice concentrate
1 tablespoon dark sesame oil
2 tablespoons rice vinegar or white-wine vinegar
1 teaspoon soy sauce

1. Rinse the spinach leaves and trim their stems. Combine them with the remaining salad ingredients in a large serving bowl.

2. Combine the dressing ingredients in a small bowl with 2 tablespoons of water and whisk together. Pour over the salad and toss well.

Calories: 111	Total fat: 2 g	Protein: 1 g
Carbohydrate: 20 g	Cholesterol: 0 g	Sodium: 86 mg

Pantry staples
❑ Quick-cooking brown rice
❑ Canola oil
❑ Dark sesame oil
❑ Onion, 1 large
❑ Cornstarch
❑ Soy sauce
❑ Rice vinegar or white-wine vinegar

Refrigerator staples
❑ Celery, 2 large stalks

Freezer staples
❑ Orange juice concentrate

Shopping list: fresh foods and nonstaples
❑ Red bell pepper, 1 large
❑ White mushrooms, about 4 ounces
❑ Fresh mung bean sprouts, ½ pound bought by weight, or 8-ounce package
❑ Baked pressed tofu, 8-ounce package
❑ Scallions, 1 bunch
❑ Vegetable stock, 1-pound can (optional)
❑ Toasted unsalted cashews, small quantity
❑ Fresh "triple-washed" spinach, 10- or 12-ounce bag
❑ Cucumber, 1 large
❑ Red cabbage, 1 head
❑ Seedless oranges such as Clementines or tangelos, 1 or 2

MENU

Easy TVP Chili

Tossed salad

Quick-cooking brown rice,
couscous, or quinoa

Steamed green vegetable (broccoli,
asparagus, or string beans)

Serves 6 to 8

TVP chili is a standby in my home, and I have relied on this simple, hearty menu many a time. TVP is available in bulk or packaged form in most natural food stores. — N. A.

Strategy:

1. Soak the TVP as directed in step 1 of the chili recipe.

2. Begin cooking the grain of your choice:

    Quick-cooking brown rice: cook a 6- or 8-serving portion according to package directions.

    Couscous: combine 1½ cups of raw grain in a heat-proof container with 3 cups of boiling water, cover for 10 to 15 minutes, then fluff with a fork.

    Quinoa: bring 3 cups of water to a boil in a large saucepan, then add 1½ cups of rinsed quinoa; cover and cook for 15 minutes, or until the water is absorbed.

EASY TVP CHILI

The first time I had TVP was years ago in a meatless chili served by a natural foods restaurant in New York City. As a vegetarian, I found the texture so disconcerting that I told our waiter that there was meat in my chili. Despite his explanation to the contrary, I remained so unconvinced that finally the owner came over to enlighten me about TVP.

So, what is TVP? It stands for texturized vegetable protein, and to describe it briefly, it is processed soy protein, all natural, and very low in fat. As I found out, it makes an uncanny substitute for ground meat.

⅔ cup raw TVP granules
2 tablespoons light olive oil
1 cup chopped onion
1 large green bell pepper, diced
2 1-pound cans pinto or pink beans, drained and
    rinsed
4-ounce can chopped mild to hot green chilies, as
    preferred
1 teaspoon ground cumin
1 teaspoon dried oregano
1 teaspoon chili powder
28-ounce can crushed or pureed tomatoes

Garnishes (all optional)
Pre-grated reduced-fat cheddar cheese
    or grated cheddar-style soy cheese
Tortilla chips, good-quality or fat-free
Reduced-fat sour cream or soy yogurt
Chunky salsa

1. Combine the TVP with ½ cup of boiling water in a heat-proof bowl and let stand until needed.

2. Heat the oil in a large soup pot. Add the onion and sauté until translucent, about 3 minutes. Add the green pepper and continue to sauté for another 5 minutes.

3. In the meantime, prepare the remaining ingredients, then add them to the pot along with ½ cup of water and the TVP. Stir, then cover and cook at a gentle but steady simmer for 15 minutes. Taste to adjust the seasonings, and add a bit more water if necessary to loosen the consistency.

4. Serve over hot cooked grain, using any — or none — of the suggested garnishes.

Variation: Add 1 cup of thawed frozen corn kernels to the chili for added color.

Calories: 251	Total fat: 5 g	Protein: 12 g
Carbohydrate: 47 g	Cholesterol: 0 g	Sodium: 47 mg

Strategy, continued

3. Continue with the chili recipe.

4. While the chili is cooking, prepare a simple tossed salad and steam a green vegetable of your choice.

Pantry staples
- ❏ Light olive oil
- ❏ Onion, 1 large or 2 medium
- ❏ Pinto or pink beans, 2 1-pound cans
- ❏ Green chilies, chopped, mild to hot as preferred, 4-ounce can
- ❏ Crushed or pureed tomatoes, 28-ounce can
- ❏ Ground cumin
- ❏ Dried oregano
- ❏ Chili powder
- ❏ Grain of your choice (quick-cooking brown rice, couscous, or quinoa)

Shopping list: fresh foods and nonstaples
- ❏ TVP granules, small quantity
- ❏ Green bell pepper, 1 large
- ❏ Salad vegetables of your choice
- ❏ Green vegetable (fresh broccoli, asparagus, or string beans)
- ❏ Pre-grated reduced-fat cheddar cheese or cheddar-style soy cheese, 8-ounce package (optional)
- ❏ Tortilla chips, good-quality or fat-free (optional)
- ❏ Reduced-fat sour cream or soy yogurt, 1-pint container (optional)
- ❏ Chunky salsa (optional)

——— MENU ———

TVP Sloppy Joes

Summer Squash and Corn Sauté

Half-sour dill pickles

Fat-free tortilla chips

Serves 6

If you are feeding any hard-core meat eaters who just won't give up their beef, this just may be the menu for you. Don't tell them that these classic sloppy joes are made of soy protein and they may not even be able to tell the difference, though the difference is very real — unlike ground beef, TVP has virtually no fat and absolutely no cholesterol.

Strategy:

1. Do steps 1 and 2 of the TVP Sloppy Joes.

2. Do step 1 of the Summer Squash and Corn Sauté.

3. Add the remaining ingredients to the sloppy joes (step 3) and simmer.

4. Do the remaining step of the squash and corn sauté.

5. Arrange pickle spears on a plate; put fat-free chips in a bowl.

TVP SLOPPY JOES

See previous menu for more information on TVP (texturized vegetable protein).

1 cup TVP granules
1 tablespoon canola or olive oil
1 medium onion, finely chopped
½ green bell pepper, finely chopped
14-ounce can crushed tomatoes or tomato puree
1 teaspoon chili powder
2 teaspoons salt-free herb-and-spice mix
1 tablespoon soy sauce
1 tablespoon light brown sugar, honey, or brown rice syrup
Whole-grain rolls or burger buns

1. Combine the TVP with 7/8 cup of boiling water in a small bowl. Let stand for 5 minutes.

2. In the meantime, heat the oil in a deep, heavy saucepan or large skillet. Add the onion and bell pepper and sauté for 4 minutes, or until tender.

3. Add the remaining ingredients except the rolls and simmer over moderate heat, covered, for 5 to 7 minutes, or until heated through. Serve on rolls or buns.

The following analysis is based on 1 serving with a roll:

Calories: 249	Total fat: 4 g	Protein: 13 g
Carbohydrate: 41 g	Cholesterol: 0 g	Sodium: 487 mg

SUMMER SQUASH AND CORN SAUTÉ

When you're not in a great hurry, using fresh, cooked corn kernels, scraped off the cob, makes this extra special. You'll need 4 to 5 large ears.

1 tablespoon olive oil
2 cloves garlic, minced
2 medium yellow summer squashes, quartered length-
    wise and sliced ¼ inch thick
1-pound bag thawed frozen corn kernels
2 medium ripe tomatoes, diced
2 to 3 scallions, minced
Salt and freshly ground pepper, to taste

1. Heat the oil plus 2 tablespoons of water in a large skillet. Add the garlic and squash and sauté over medium-high heat until the squash is tender-crisp, about 5 to 7 minutes.

2. Add the remaining ingredients and sauté 5 to 7 minutes more, or until the tomatoes are slightly softened and the mixture is heated through.

Calories: 249	Total fat: 4 g	Protein: 13 g
Carbohydrate: 41 g	Cholesterol: 0 g	Sodium: 487 mg

Pantry staples
❏ Olive oil
❏ Canola oil (optional)
❏ Onion, 1 medium
❏ Crushed or pureed tomatoes, 14-ounce can
❏ Chili powder
❏ Salt-free herb-and-spice seasoning mix
❏ Soy sauce
❏ Light brown sugar, honey, or brown rice syrup

Refrigerator staples
❏ Fresh garlic

Freezer staples
❏ Frozen corn kernels, 1-pound bag

Shopping list: fresh foods and nonstaples
❏ TVP granules, small quantity
❏ Green bell pepper, 1 medium
❏ Yellow summer squashes, 2
❏ Tomatoes, 2 medium
❏ Scallions, 1 bunch
❏ Fresh whole-grain rolls or burger buns, 6
❏ Half-sour dill pickles
❏ Fat-free tortilla chips

MENU

Southern Ranch-Style Beans with "Frankfurters"

Steamed broccoli

Simple coleslaw

Fresh rye bread

Serves 6 to 8

This is desperation cookery at its best; both of us rely on this menu often when dinner has to be on the table in a hurry.

Strategy:

1. Do step 1 of the recipe for Southern Ranch-Style Beans.

2. While the onions sauté, combine a 1-pound bag of pre-shredded cole-slaw cabbage with reduced-fat mayonnaise or sour cream, commercially prepared tofu mayonnaise, or a bottled reduced-fat dressing of your choice. If time allows, add some fresh bell pepper strips. Toss well and set aside.

3. Complete the recipe for Southern Ranch-Style Beans.

4. While the beans simmer, steam about a pound of broccoli florets in a large pot with about an inch of water until bright green and tender-crisp. Drain and transfer them to a

SOUTHERN RANCH-STYLE BEANS WITH "FRANKFURTERS"

You might have to compare brands before you find the tofu hot dogs you like best, as some are far superior to others in terms of flavor, texture, and resemblance to the real thing. Our favorite brand, Yves, available in natural food stores, fools everyone with its excellent texture and perfect seasoning, and it even comes in a completely fat-free version.

Southern Ranch-Style Beans is a mouthwatering, sweet-sour dish, and with the addition of good-quality tofu hot dogs it becomes a sort of new and improved version of the old classic, franks and beans.

1 tablespoon canola oil
2 medium onions, halved and thinly sliced
2 1-pound cans vegetarian-style baked beans with liquid
1-pound can kidney or red beans, drained and rinsed
⅓ cup light brown sugar
2 teaspoons prepared mustard
1 tablespoon apple cider vinegar
6 good-quality tofu hot dogs, sliced

1. Heat the oil in a large pot with 2 tablespoons of water. Add the onions and sauté over moderate heat, covered, for 5 minutes, stirring occasionally.

2. Add the remaining ingredients and bring to a simmer. Cover and cook at a gentle but steady simmer for about 15 minutes. Serve in bowls.

Calories: 324	Total fat: 4 g	Protein: 17 g
Carbohydrate: 52 g	Cholesterol: 0 g	Sodium: 560 mg

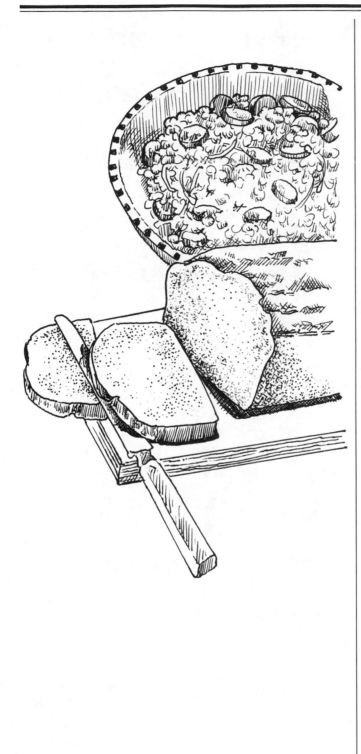

Strategy, continued

covered serving dish. Add a teaspoon or two of butter or margarine, if desired.

5. Slice the fresh rye bread and arrange it on a plate.

6. Serve the ranch beans in small bowls set atop plates, and at the same time, pass around the bread, coleslaw, and broccoli.

Pantry staples
- ❑ Canola oil
- ❑ Onions, 2 medium
- ❑ Kidney or red beans, 1-pound can
- ❑ Light brown sugar
- ❑ Apple cider vinegar

Refrigerator staples
- ❑ Prepared mustard
- ❑ Reduced-fat mayonnaise, reduced-fat sour cream, or commercially prepared tofu mayonnaise

Shopping list: fresh foods and nonstaples
- ❑ Vegetarian-style baked beans, 2 1-pound cans
- ❑ Tofu hot dogs, package of 6 or more
- ❑ Broccoli, 2 medium bunches or 1 pound fresh precut florets
- ❑ Pre-shredded coleslaw cabbage, 1-pound bag
- ❑ Fresh rye bread, 1 loaf

Chapter Six

SALAD DAYS

A meal of salad can be ideal for warm weather, or really any time that you prefer something on the lighter side. But we don't think of salad as rabbit food — some of the following selections are quite sturdy. Most of these salad meals are based on pasta, grains, beans, or a combination, so they make for very hearty cold fare. And some have so much visual appeal — Aztec Platter or Salade Niçoise, for instance — that they can be prime choices when you need to put together a quick meal for company.

Nineteenth-century American essayist Charles Dudley Warner wrote, "You can put everything, and the more things the better, into a salad… but everything depends on the skill of mixing." We've simplified the skill of mixing here so that you can enjoy bountiful salad meals in a flash.

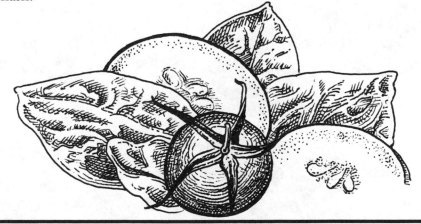

Cold Noodles with Hot Chili-Orange Oil
Sesame Cucumber Salad

Asian Noodle Salad
Indonesian Vegetable Salad with Spicy Peanut Dressing

Rotini with Beans and Corn
Wilted Sesame Spinach
Fresh whole-grain bread or rolls

Tortellini Capri
Gazpacho Salad
Fresh Italian or French Bread

Greengrocer's Ziti Salad
Green salad with lemon juice and olive oil
Biscuits or fresh rolls with nut butter

Aztec Platter
(Composed Quinoa, Corn, and Bean Salad)
Microwaved sweet potatoes

Main-Dish Couscous Salad
Spiced Chickpeas
Warm pita bread

Warm and Hearty Two-Rice Salad
Waldorf Salad
Hot cornbread (purchased)

Salade Niçoise with Tofu Mock Tuna
Red-Skinned Potatoes with Yogurt and Chives
Breadsticks

Antipasto, Vegetarian Style
Fresh Italian bread

_____ MENU _____

Cold Noodles with Hot Chili-
Orange Oil

Sesame Cucumber Salad

Serves 6

_____

Despite its speedy preparation, this light meal is elegant enough for a special occasion. All it takes is a little advance planning so you'll have the ingredients on hand. Special occasion or not, save it for someone you really want to impress. Or go ahead and impress yourself.

_____

Strategy:

1. Prepare the cucumber salad and set aside.

2. Prepare the cold noodle salad.

COLD NOODLES WITH HOT CHILI-ORANGE OIL

10 to 12 ounces angel hair pasta (cappellini)
8-ounce package fresh bean sprouts
2 large carrots, coarsely grated in food processor
6 scallions, sliced thinly on the diagonal
¼ cup chopped fresh parsley, or more or less to taste, divided

Dressing
1 tablespoon Oriental hot chili oil, or to taste, or 1 tablespoon dark sesame oil plus 1 to 2 teaspoons chili powder
2 to 3 tablespoons soy sauce, or to taste
¼ cup rice vinegar or white-wine vinegar
2 tablespoons sugar
2 tablespoons undiluted orange juice concentrate

Garnishes
½ cup dry-roasted peanuts, coarsely crushed, for garnish
1 or 2 seedless oranges (such as Clementines or tangelos), peeled and sectioned (optional)

1. Cook the angel hair pasta until *al dente*. When it's done, drain and rinse it under cold water until it's cool, and transfer it to a large bowl.

2. In the meantime, place the bean sprouts in a steamer basket over an inch or so of water in a large saucepan. Steam them over medium-high heat, covered, until they're just wilted, about 2 to 3 minutes. Alternatively, simply place them in a saucepan with a half inch of water and steam, covered, for 2 to 3 minutes. Drain and rinse them under cold water until they're cool.

3. Prepare the carrots, scallions, and parsley as directed (reserve half of the parsley for garnish); combine them in a large bowl with the cooked and cooled pasta and the steamed sprouts.

4. In a small bowl, combine the dressing ingredients and pour the dressing over the pasta mixture. Toss well to coat all the strands, then garnish the top with the reserved parsley and chopped peanuts. Pass around a plate of seedless orange sections to serve alongside, if desired.

Calories: 242	Total fat: 6 g	Protein: 9 g
Carbohydrate: 38 g	Cholesterol: 0 g	Sodium: 393 mg

SESAME CUCUMBER SALAD

Because English cucumbers are virtually seedless, they always seem crisp and flavorful. They are becoming widely available at produce outlets and supermarkets, sometimes marketed simply as "seedless cucumbers" or more amusingly, "burpless cucumbers." They are about twice the length of ordinary cucumbers and are unwaxed, so you need not peel them.

1 long English seedless cucumber, unpeeled
2 tablespoons canola oil
2½ tablespoons rice vinegar
2 teaspoons light soy sauce
1 teaspoon honey or brown rice syrup
1 to 2 teaspoons grated fresh ginger, to taste
2 tablespoons toasted sesame seeds

1. Use the ultra-thin slicing blade of a food processor to slice the cucumber, peel and all, or slice it very thinly by hand.

2. In a small mixing bowl, combine the oil, vinegar, soy sauce, and honey or rice syrup. Stir to mix thoroughly, then stir in the ginger. Pour the oil and vinegar mixture over the cucumber slices and toss well, then sprinkle the sesame seeds over the top.

Calories: 70	Total fat: 6 g	Protein: 1 g
Carbohydrate: 3 g	Cholesterol: 0 g	Sodium: 113 mg

Pantry staples
❑ Canola oil
❑ Soy sauce
❑ Rice vinegar or white-wine vinegar
❑ Honey or brown rice syrup
❑ Angel hair pasta (cappellini), 1-pound package

Refrigerator staples
❑ Carrots, 2 large

Freezer staples
❑ Orange juice concentrate

Shopping list: fresh foods and nonstaples
❑ Seedless English cucumber, 1 long
❑ Fresh bean sprouts, ½ pound bought by weight, or 8-ounce package
❑ Dry-roasted peanuts, small quantity
❑ Fresh parsley, 1 bunch
❑ Scallions, 1 bunch
❑ Fresh ginger
❑ Oriental hot chili oil (if unavailable, substitute dark sesame oil plus chili powder)
❑ Toasted sesame seeds, small quantity
❑ Small seedless oranges such as Clementines or tangelos, 6 (optional)

Asian Noodle Salad

Indonesian Vegetable Salad with
Spicy Peanut Dressing

Serves 6

*Here's a menu that's offbeat and exotic, but
not so far off the mainstream that it can't
be a real crowd pleaser. With a myriad of
flavors, textures, and colors, it's a wonderful cold meal with an Asian twist.*

Strategy:

1. Prepare the Asian Noodle Salad.

2. Prepare the Indonesian Vegetable
   Salad.

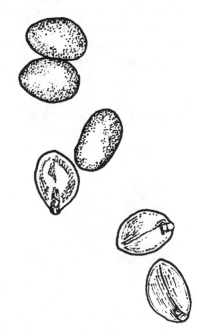

ASIAN NOODLE SALAD

½ pound udon or soba noodles (see Note)
¼ to ½ cup fresh parsley or cilantro leaves
   (remove thicker stems, but don't be fussy about
   smaller ones)
3 scallions, coarsely chopped
2 tablespoons soy sauce
2 tablespoons dark sesame oil
1 tablespoon lemon juice
1 small fresh green chili, such as jalapeño or serrano,
   chopped (optional)

1. Begin cooking the noodles according to package directions.

2. In the meantime, combine the remaining ingredients
in a food processor fitted with a steel blade. Process until
the herbs are very finely minced.

3. When the noodles are done, drain and rinse them under cool water until they are at room temperature. Drain
them well again, then combine them with the sauce in a
serving bowl and toss well.

Note: Soba and udon noodles are delicious whole-grain
noodles that are readily available in all natural food stores.
If necessary, however, you may substitute spaghetti or
linguine.

Calories: 97	Total fat: 5 g	Protein: 3 g
Carbohydrate: 11 g	Cholesterol: 0 g	Sodium: 339 mg

INDONESIAN VEGETABLE SALAD WITH SPICY PEANUT DRESSING

½ pound baby carrots
½ pound precut broccoli florets

8-ounce package fresh mung bean sprouts
½ medium cucumber, sliced
1 small red bell pepper, cut into strips
4 ounces (1 small cake or ¼ of a 1-pound package) extra-firm tofu, diced

Dressing
¼ cup peanut butter, at room temperature
2 tablespoons rice vinegar or white-wine vinegar
2 tablespoons light brown sugar
1 teaspoon chili powder, or more to taste
½ teaspoon salt
¼ cup dry-roasted peanut halves for topping

1. In a large saucepan or soup pot, layer the carrots, then the broccoli, then the bean sprouts. Add about an inch of water, then steam them, covered, for 4 to 5 minutes, or until the broccoli is bright green and the sprouts are slightly wilted.

2. While the vegetables steam, prepare the cucumber, red pepper, and tofu.

3. When the steamed vegetables are ready, drain them and rinse them under cool water until they are at room temperature. Drain them well again, transfer them to a serving bowl, and combine them with the cucumber, red pepper, and tofu.

4. Combine all the dressing ingredients except the peanuts with 3 tablespoons of hot water in a small bowl and whisk them together until smooth. Pour the dressing over the vegetables and toss gently but thoroughly to combine.

5. Scatter peanut halves over the top and serve.

Calories: 169	Total fat: 8 g	Protein: 7 g
Carbohydrate: 16 g	Cholesterol: 0 g	Sodium: 221 mg

Pantry staples
❑ Soy sauce
❑ Dark sesame oil
❑ Peanut butter
❑ Chili powder
❑ Rice vinegar or white-wine vinegar
❑ Light brown sugar

Refrigerator staples
❑ Lemon, 1

Shopping list: fresh foods and nonstaples
❑ Udon or soba noodles, 8-ounce package
❑ Fresh parsley or cilantro, 1 small bunch
❑ Scallions, 1 bunch
❑ Fresh jalapeño or serrano chili, 1 (optional)
❑ Cucumber, 1 medium
❑ Red bell pepper, 1 small
❑ Baby carrots, 1 small package
❑ Mung bean sprouts, 8-ounce package
❑ Broccoli florets, precut, ½ pound
❑ Extra-firm tofu, 4-ounce cake or portion of 1-pound tub
❑ Dry-roasted peanuts, small quantity

MENU

Rotini with Beans and Corn

Wilted Sesame Spinach

Fresh whole-grain bread or rolls

Serves 8

If you make it a habit to keep a few varieties of beans on hand, you'll be ready to assemble hearty main-dish salads such as this one any time. Black beans and chick peas combine with frozen corn and rotini pasta to make this winning combination.

Strategy:

1. Cook the pasta for the rotini salad.

2. Prepare the Wilted Sesame Spinach.

3. Finish preparing the rotini salad.

ROTINI WITH BEANS AND CORN

½ pound rotini (corkscrew) pasta
10-ounce package (2 cups) frozen corn,
    thoroughly thawed
1 cup canned black beans, rinsed and drained
1 cup canned chickpeas, rinsed and drained
1 medium green bell pepper, diced
1 small red onion, thinly sliced, or 2 scallions, minced
8 to 10 oil-cured sun-dried tomatoes,
    drained and sliced
½ to ¾ cup bottled low-fat Italian dressing, as needed
Salt and freshly ground pepper, to taste
6 to 8 large leaves fresh basil, thinly sliced, if available
½ cup chopped fresh parsley, or a combination of
    parsley and dill, to taste

1. Bring a large pot of water to a rolling boil, add the pasta and cook at a steady simmer until *al dente*. Drain the pasta, rinse it under cold water to cool, and drain again.

2. Combine the cooked pasta with the corn, black beans, chickpeas, bell pepper, onion or scallions, and dried tomatoes, and toss. Add enough dressing to moisten and flavor the salad to taste. Season to taste with salt and plenty of freshly ground pepper and toss well.

3. Add the fresh herbs and toss again.

Helpful tip: Combine the black beans and chickpeas remaining from their cans in a small storage container, freeze, and thaw at a later time for use in salad or as a side dish.

Calories: 188	Total fat: 4 g	Protein: 6 g
Carbohydrate: 31 g	Cholesterol: 0 g	Sodium: 332 mg

WILTED SESAME SPINACH

Fresh spinach is now widely available in packages marked "triple-washed." Though it is still a good idea to rinse it, using this type of clean spinach dispenses with the tedious washing generally associated with fresh spinach, not to mention the risk of getting a mouthful of sand!

12-ounce package fresh "triple-washed" spinach,
    stemmed and rinsed
1 tablespoon soy sauce
1 teaspoon dark sesame oil
1 teaspoon canola or other vegetable oil
1 tablespoon lemon juice
Freshly ground pepper, to taste
1 tablespoon toasted sesame seeds

1. Remove the stems from the spinach leaves and rinse them.

2. Place the spinach in a large pot, cover, and steam, using just the water clinging to the leaves, for 2 to 3 minutes, until they are just lightly wilted. Transfer the wilted spinach to a serving bowl.

3. Combine the soy sauce, oils, and lemon juice in a small bowl and mix. Pour the mixture over the spinach and toss. Add a few grindings of pepper, and toss again. Top with the sesame seeds and serve at room temperature.

Calories: 28	Total fat: 2 g	Protein: 1 g
Carbohydrate: 2 g	Cholesterol: 0 g	Sodium: 159 mg

Pantry staples
❏ Black beans, 1-pound can
❏ Chickpeas, 1-pound can
❏ Soy sauce
❏ Dark sesame oil
❏ Canola or other vegetable oil
❏ Sesame seeds
❏ Onion, 1 small red

Refrigerator staples
❏ Low-fat Italian dressing
❏ Lemon, 1
❏ Fresh garlic

Freezer staples
❏ Frozen corn, 10-ounce package

Shopping list: fresh foods and nonstaples
❏ Rotini (corkscrew) pasta, 1-pound package
❏ Green bell pepper, 1 medium
❏ Fresh "triple-washed" spinach, 12-ounce package
❏ Oil-cured sun-dried tomatoes, about 4 ounces
❏ Fresh basil, 1 small bunch, if available
❏ Fresh parsley and/or dill, 1 bunch
❏ Fresh whole-grain bread, 1 loaf, or whole-grain rolls, 8

MENU

Tortellini Capri

Gazpacho Salad

Fresh Italian or French bread

Serves 6

This delectable pasta salad makes for a cold main dish that's simple enough to make as an everyday meal, yet special enough to serve to company. It's accompanied by a salad comprising the refreshing flavors of gazpacho, a classic cold soup. Here the vegetables are not blended, as they would be for the soup, but rather served diced and dressed with a spicy, fat-free dressing.

Strategy:

1. Begin cooking the tortellini.

2. Prepare the vegetables for the tortellini salad.

3. While the tortellini are still cooking, prepare the Gazpacho Salad.

4. Assemble the tortellini salad.

TORTELLINI CAPRI

1 pound good-quality frozen cheese tortellini or vegetable-filled tortellini
1 cup unthawed frozen green peas
2 cups finely chopped fresh broccoli florets
10- or 12-ounce jar roasted red peppers

Dressing
Juices from the roasted peppers
2 tablespoons olive oil, preferably extra-virgin
2 tablespoons red-wine vinegar
2 teaspoons Dijon-style mustard
¼ cup grated fresh Parmesan cheese
Salt and freshly ground pepper, to taste

1. Begin cooking the tortellini according to package directions.

2. Layer the frozen peas and the broccoli florets in a large saucepan with ½ inch of water. Bring them to a simmer and steam over moderate heat, covered, until the peas are thawed and the broccoli is bright green, about 3 to 4 minutes. Drain the peas and broccoli and rinse them under cool water until they are at room temperature.

3. In the meantime, drain the roasted peppers, reserving the juices in a small mixing bowl. Cut the peppers into strips.

4. Combine the red-pepper juices with the remaining dressing ingredients and mix.

5. When the tortellini are done, drain them and rinse under cool water until they are at room temperature. Combine them in a mixing bowl with the peas, broccoli, red pepper strips, and dressing. Add the Parmesan cheese and toss well. Season to taste with salt and pepper and toss again.

Calories: 204	Total fat: 10 g	Protein: 9 g
Carbohydrate: 19 g	Cholesterol: 11 g	Sodium: 327 mg

GAZPACHO SALAD

1 medium green bell pepper, diced
1 medium red bell pepper, diced
1 large cucumber, peeled if necessary, then quartered
    lengthwise and chopped
2 large ripe tomatoes, diced
5 to 6 radishes, sliced
2 tablespoons chopped fresh dill

Dressing
¾ cup canned crushed tomatoes or tomato puree
Juice of ½ lemon
1 teaspoon chili powder
Dash of salt (optional)
Freshly ground pepper, to taste

1. In a serving bowl, preferably one with deep, straight sides (a glass one is nice, too, to show all the layers of vegetables), layer the vegetables and dill in the order given, but do not toss.

2. Combine all the dressing ingredients in a small bowl and mix well. Drizzle the dressing over the salad. To serve, take deep scoops with a large serving spoon.

Calories: 35	Total fat: 0 g	Protein: 1 g
Carbohydrate: 7 g	Cholesterol: 0 g	Sodium: 18 mg

Pantry staples
❏ Olive oil (preferably extra-virgin)
❏ 8-ounce can crushed tomatoes or tomato puree (or portion of 14-ounce can)
❏ Red-wine vinegar
❏ Chili powder

Refrigerator staples
❏ Grated Parmesan cheese
❏ Lemon, 1
❏ Dijon-style mustard

Freezer staples
❏ Frozen green peas, portion of 10-ounce package or 1-pound bag

Shopping list: fresh foods and nonstaples
❏ Frozen cheese-filled or vegetable-filled tortellini, 1-pound bag
❏ Fresh broccoli, preferably precut florets, about ½ pound
❏ Roasted red peppers, 10- or 12-ounce jar
❏ Green bell pepper, 1 medium
❏ Red bell pepper, 1 medium
❏ Cucumber, 1 large
❏ Tomatoes, 2 large
❏ Radishes, 1 small bunch or package
❏ Fresh dill, 1 small bunch
❏ Fresh Italian or French bread

ꟿ𝓔𝓝𝓤

Greengrocer's Ziti Salad

Green salad with lemon juice and olive oil

Biscuits or fresh rolls with nut butter

Serves 6 to 8

Some main-dish salads are so complete in and of themselves that they need little more to accompany them than a simple green salad. This is one of them. Serve the fresh biscuits or rolls with a jar of nut butter (peanut or cashew, or for the even more adventurous, pistachio or almond) to round out the complement of proteins.

Strategy:

1. Cook the ziti. While it's cooking, prepare the vegetables and make the dressing.

2. At odd moments, prepare a simple salad of mixed greens. Dress lightly with olive oil and lemon juice.

3. Assemble the ziti salad.

4. Warm the biscuits or rolls, if desired, and serve with one or two varieties of nut butter, such as peanut, cashew, or almond.

GREENGROCER'S ZITI SALAD

10 to 12 ounces ziti pasta (penne may be substituted)
1 medium red onion, very thinly sliced
4 firm ripe plum tomatoes, diced
¾ cup diced sweet pickles
2 medium green bell peppers, diced
10-ounce package soft silken tofu
2 tablespoons lemon juice (about ½ lemon)
½ cup reduced-fat mayonnaise or commercially prepared tofu mayonnaise
¼ cup chopped fresh dill, or 1 tablespoon dried dill
Salt and freshly ground pepper, to taste

1. Cook the pasta in a large pot of steadily boiling water until *al dente*. When it's done, drain and rinse it under cold water; drain it well again.

2. While the pasta cooks, prepare the onions, tomatoes, sweet pickles, and bell peppers, and place them in a serving bowl.

3. In a food processor fitted with a steel blade, combine the silken tofu, lemon juice, and mayonnaise. Process until smooth.

4. Combine the pasta with the vegetables and the tofu dressing. Add the fresh or dried dill and toss gently but thoroughly. Season to taste with salt, if desired, and freshly ground pepper, and serve.

Calories: 168	Total fat: 7 g	Protein: 5 g
Carbohydrate: 21 g	Cholesterol: 6 g	Sodium: 120 mg

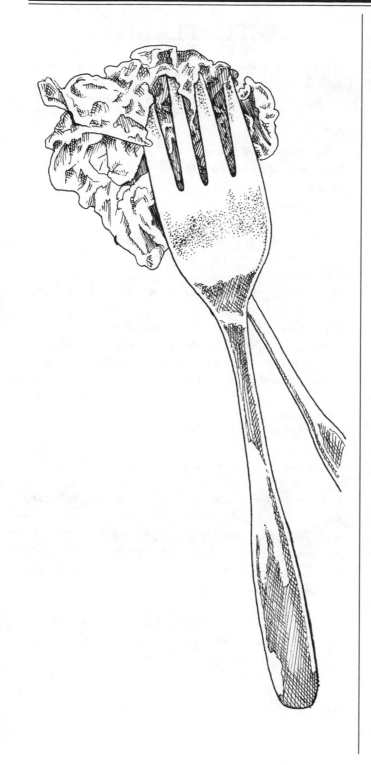

Pantry staples
- ❏ Onion, 1 medium red
- ❏ Peanut and/or other nut butters such as cashew or almond
- ❏ Olive oil

Refrigerator staples
- ❏ Lemon, 1
- ❏ Reduced-fat mayonnaise or commercially prepared tofu mayonnaise

Shopping list: fresh foods and nonstaples
- ❏ Ziti, 1-pound box (penne may be substituted)
- ❏ Plum tomatoes, 4 medium
- ❏ Green bell peppers, 2 medium
- ❏ Soft silken (aseptic-packed) tofu, 10-ounce package
- ❏ Fresh or dried dill weed
- ❏ Sweet pickles, small jar
- ❏ Salad greens of your choice
- ❏ Biscuits or fresh rolls, 8

𝓜ENU

**Aztec Platter
(Composed Quinoa, Corn, and
Bean Salad)**

Microwaved sweet potatoes

Serves 6

This composed salad meal features quinoa, a grain known for having been a staple food of the ancient Aztecs of South America. Fairly recently revived for the North American natural foods market, quinoa has a nutritional profile superior among grains, with high-quality protein and an abundance of vitamins and minerals. With a distinctive yet mild flavor and aroma, quinoa cooks to a light, fluffy texture in only 15 minutes, making it a great quick grain. Quinoa is widely available in natural food stores, and now even in some supermarkets, packaged in small boxes.

Strategy:

1. Place 6 medium scrubbed sweet potatoes in the microwave, set at enough time per potato according to the wattage of your unit, and bake. If your unit is less than 750 watts, you may need to bake half of the sweet potatoes at a time and serve everyone a half. Then bake the rest and serve as a second helping later

AZTEC PLATTER

This attractive composed salad is a nourishing meal in and of itself. It can wow company, but at the same time it's simple and fast enough to prepare for an everyday meal.

Quinoa-corn salad
1 cup quinoa, well rinsed
1 cup thawed frozen corn kernels
Juice of 1 lemon
1 tablespoon olive oil
2 or 3 scallions, minced
Salt and freshly ground pepper, to taste

Bean salad
1-pound can pinto, pink, or kidney beans, drained and
  rinsed
1 heaping cup finely diced ripe tomatoes
1 tablespoon apple cider vinegar or balsamic vinegar
¼ cup chopped fresh parsley, or more or less to taste
Freshly ground pepper, to taste

Garnishes
Pumpkin seeds
Black olives
1 medium red bell pepper, cut into strips

1. Bring 2 cups of water to a boil in a heavy saucepan. Add the quinoa and simmer gently, covered, for 15 minutes. When the quinoa is done, remove it from the heat, fluff it with a fork, and transfer it to a mixing bowl. Combine the quinoa with the remaining ingredients for the quinoa-corn salad and toss well.

2. While the quinoa is cooking, combine all the ingredients for the bean salad in another bowl and toss together.

3. To assemble the Aztec Platter, transfer the quinoa-corn salad onto a large platter and spread evenly to within an inch or so of the edge. Pushing the salad outward from the center, make a well in the center of the platter about 5 inches in diameter. Mound the bean salad into the well, and sprinkle it with a handful of pumpkin seeds.

4. Arrange olives and pepper strips around the edge of the platter.

Calories: 233	Total fat: 4 g	Protein: 9 g
Carbohydrate: 40 g	Cholesterol: 0 g	Sodium: 9 mg

Strategy, continued

in the meal. Otherwise all 6 potatoes might not be done within the allotted time.

2. Prepare the Aztec Platter.

Pantry staples
❑ Olive oil
❑ Pinto, pink, or kidney beans, 1-pound can
❑ Apple cider vinegar or balsamic vinegar
❑ Black olives, 8-ounce or 1-pound can

Refrigerator staples
❑ Lemon, 1

Freezer staples
❑ Corn kernels, portion of 10-ounce package or 1-pound bag

Shopping list: fresh foods and nonstaples
❑ Quinoa, 12-ounce box
❑ Scallions, 1 bunch
❑ Ripe tomatoes, about 2 medium
❑ Parsley, 1 small bunch
❑ Pumpkin seeds, small quantity
❑ Red bell pepper, 1 medium
❑ Sweet potatoes, 6 medium

MENU

Main-Dish Couscous Salad

Spiced Chickpeas

Warm pita bread

Serves 6

Couscous, an important staple in North African and Moroccan cuisines, is readily available in small boxes in most American supermarkets, and in economical bulk form in every natural food store. It needs only to be soaked in boiling water for 10 minutes. Inspired by the traditional ingredients of the North African stew simply known as couscous, this simple salad duo makes for hearty cold fare.

Strategy:

1. Prepare the couscous salad.

2. Wrap 6 pita breads in foil and warm them in a 300-degree oven or toaster oven.

3. Prepare the Spiced Chickpeas.

MAIN-DISH COUSCOUS SALAD

1½ cups couscous
1 small package (2 cups) fresh carrot sticks,
    cut into 1-inch lengths
1 small white turnip, cut into sticks
1 medium red bell pepper, cut into 1-inch dice
1 medium zucchini, cut into quarters and then
    1-inch chunks
2 medium tomatoes, diced
3 tablespoons light olive oil
Juice of 1 large lemon, or more to taste
1 teaspoon ground cumin
Salt and freshly ground pepper, to taste
Fresh cilantro, minced (optional)

1. Cover the couscous with 3 cups of boiling water in a heat-proof dish. Cover and let stand for 10 minutes.

2. In the meantime, prepare the vegetables as directed. When the couscous has absorbed all the water, fluff it with a fork, then combine it with the vegetables and remaining ingredients in a serving bowl. Toss the salad well to combine.

Helpful tip: If the salad stands for some time, or if you are serving leftovers, add a few drops of water to it to loosen the consistency if it has gotten dense.

Calories: 227	Total fat: 7 g	Protein: 5 g
Carbohydrate: 36 g	Cholesterol: 0 g	Sodium: 54 mg

SPICED CHICKPEAS

2 1-pound cans chickpeas, rinsed and drained
2 tablespoons olive oil
Juice of ½ lemon
¼ cup chopped scallions
1 clove garlic, minced
½ teaspoon ground cumin
¼ teaspoon cinnamon
¼ teaspoon ground coriander
Dark green lettuce leaves

1. Combine all of the ingredients except the lettuce in a serving bowl and toss well.

2. Place each serving on a bed of lettuce.

Variation: Add a small amount of crumbled feta cheese to the salad.

Calories: 220	Total fat: 7 g	Protein: 8 g
Carbohydrate: 31 g	Cholesterol: 0 g	Sodium: 8 mg

Pantry staples
❑ Olive oil
❑ Ground cumin
❑ Ground coriander
❑ Cinnamon
❑ Chickpeas, 2 1-pound cans

Refrigerator staples
❑ Lemons, 2
❑ Fresh garlic

Shopping list: fresh foods and nonstaples
❑ Carrot sticks, 1 small (2-cup) package
❑ White turnip, 1 small
❑ Red bell pepper, 1 medium
❑ Zucchini, 1 medium
❑ Tomatoes, 2 medium
❑ Couscous, 14-ounce box, or about 1 pound if bought in bulk
❑ Scallions, 1 bunch
❑ Cilantro, 1 small bunch (optional)
❑ Dark green lettuce such as romaine
❑ Pita breads

MENU

Warm and Hearty Two-Rice Salad

Waldorf Salad

Hot cornbread (purchased)

Serves 6

This is a hearty salad that comes loaded with just about everything that's good for you. And it goes together in a snap, thanks to quick-cooking brown and wild rices available in supermarkets. However, you don't have to tell the family just how easy it was. Let them believe you went to a lot of trouble.

Strategy:

1. Cook the brown and wild rices separately, according to package directions.

2. While they cool, prepare the remaining ingredients for the rice salad and set aside.

3. Place purchased cornbread, covered with foil, in a 300-degree oven to warm.

4. Prepare the Waldorf Salad.

5. Finish assembling the rice salad.

WARM AND HEARTY TWO-RICE SALAD

6-serving portion quick-cooking brown rice
2¾-ounce box instant wild rice
½ pound extra-firm tofu, diced
10-ounce package frozen green peas, thawed
4 scallions, white and green, sliced
½ cup finely diced red bell pepper

Dressing
2 tablespoons canola oil
¼ cup tarragon vinegar (if unavailable, use white-wine vinegar)
2 tablespoons Dijon mustard
Salt, to taste
½ teaspoon freshly ground pepper

Dark green lettuce leaves

1. Following package directions, prepare the brown rice and the wild rice in separate saucepans. Turn them out into a large bowl to cool.

2. While the rice is cooling, prepare the tofu, peas, scallions, and bell pepper.

3. In a small bowl, whisk together the dressing ingredients.

4. In a large salad bowl, combine the two rices with the remaining salad ingredients and the dressing and toss well. Serve in a lettuce-lined bowl or on individual lettuce-lined plates.

Calories: 305	Total fat: 10 g	Protein: 8 g
Carbohydrate: 44 g	Cholesterol: 0 g	Sodium: 167 mg

WALDORF SALAD

2 tablespoons lemon juice
4 medium Golden Delicious apples, cored and diced
4 medium stalks celery
¾ cup coarsely chopped walnuts
⅓ to ½ cup reduced-calorie mayonnaise or
   commercially prepared tofu mayonnaise

1. Combine the lemon juice with enough cool water to fill a medium-sized mixing bowl. Set aside. Quarter the apples and core them. Cut them into small dice, dropping the pieces into the lemon water as they're cut.

2. Finely dice the celery and chop the walnuts. Drain the apples very well and return them to the mixing bowl. Add the celery, walnuts, and just enough mayonnaise to coat the ingredients.

Variation: Though mayonnaise is traditional to a Waldorf salad, you may substitute plain, low-fat yogurt or soy yogurt.

Calories: 193	Total fat: 12 g	Protein: 2 g
Carbohydrate: 18 g	Cholesterol: 4 g	Sodium: 105 mg

Pantry staples
❏ Quick-cooking brown rice
❏ Canola oil

Freezer staples
❏ Frozen green peas, 10-ounce package or portion of 1-pound bag

Refrigerator staples
❏ Reduced-calorie mayonnaise or commercially prepared tofu mayonnaise
❏ Dijon mustard
❏ Lemon, 1

Shopping list: fresh foods and nonstaples
❏ Extra-firm tofu, ½ pound
❏ Golden Delicious apples, 4 medium
❏ Celery
❏ Chopped walnuts, small quantity
❏ Instant wild rice, 2¾-ounce box
❏ Red bell pepper, 1 small
❏ Dark green lettuce, 1 head
❏ Scallions, 1 bunch
❏ Tarragon vinegar (if unavailable, substitute white-wine vinegar)
❏ Cornbread

A fine Italian touch of ripe tomatoes, ol-ives, and "tuna" is evident in this classic main-dish salad which originated in Nice. Of course, we've substituted baked pressed tofu for tuna, but the sunny flavors remain intact. Also, since this is what's called a salade composé, don't toss it until after everyone has had a chance to admire it.

Strategy:

1. Prepare the potatoes as directed in step 1 of the recipe.

2. Prepare the Salade Niçoise.

3. Complete the potato recipe.

SALADE NIÇOISE WITH TOFU MOCK TUNA

Baked pressed tofu has a firm, chewy texture and a delicious, slightly salty flavor, making it a great stand-in for tuna. It is readily available in 8-ounce packages at natural food stores.

1 large red onion, thinly sliced
½ cup bottled red-wine vinegar and oil salad dressing, preferably low-fat, plus a little extra
10-ounce package frozen green beans
1 large head Boston lettuce, torn in pieces
8-ounce package baked pressed tofu, diced
6 firm, ripe plum tomatoes, quartered
14-ounce can artichoke hearts, drained and cut into large, bite-sized pieces
1-pound can cannellini or great Northern beans, drained and rinsed
4 ounces black olives, preferably brine-cured
1 garlic clove, mashed and minced
1 teaspoon Dijon-style mustard
¼ cup mixed chopped fresh basil and parsley

1. Place the onion slices in a small bowl, pour the red-wine vinegar dressing over them, and set aside to marinate.

2. Blanch or microwave the green beans until they are bright green and tender-crisp. Drain and rinse them until they're at room temperature.

3. Drain the red onion, reserving the dressing in a small bowl.

4. In a deep and wide round platter or bowl, arrange the lettuce to make a bed. Arrange the tofu to form a pie-wedge shape, then make another wedge of the tomato quarters, another each of the green beans, artichoke hearts, white beans, and red onion. Arrange the black olives in a small mound in the center.

5. In a small bowl, combine the reserved dressing plus enough additional red-wine vinegar dressing to make ½ cup. Add the garlic, mustard, and mixed herbs to the dressing. Whisk with a fork and drizzle over the salad.

6. Let everyone ooh and aah over the salad, then toss it well and serve.

Calories: 211	Total fat: 6 g	Protein: 10 g
Carbohydrate: 30 g	Cholesterol: 0 g	Sodium: 216 mg

RED-SKINNED POTATOES WITH YOGURT AND CHIVES

6 medium red-skinned potatoes or 18 tiny new potatoes
8-ounce container plain low-fat yogurt (or substitute reduced-fat sour cream)
Freeze-dried chives or fresh chives

1. Scrub the potatoes. If using medium-sized potatoes, cut them into quarters. If using new potatoes, cut them in half. Place the potatoes in a deep, heavy saucepan, cover them with water, and bring them to a simmer, covered. Cook the potatoes at a steady simmer until tender but still firm, about 10 to 12 minutes.

2. Drain the potatoes and transfer them to a shallow serving bowl. Top them with the yogurt, then sprinkle them with chives.

Calories: 247	Total fat: 1 g	Protein: 6 g
Carbohydrate: 54 g	Cholesterol: 3 g	Sodium: 46 mg

Pantry staples
❑ Red onion, 1 large
❑ Cannellini or great Northern beans, 1-pound can
❑ Freeze-dried chives (if not using fresh)

Refrigerator staples
❑ Fresh garlic
❑ Dijon-style mustard
❑ Plain, low-fat yogurt

Shopping list: fresh foods and nonstaples
❑ Baked pressed tofu, 8-ounce package
❑ Reduced-fat red-wine vinegar and oil salad dressing, 1 bottle
❑ Boston lettuce, 1 large head
❑ Plum or Roma tomatoes, 6 medium
❑ Frozen cut green beans, 10-ounce package
❑ Artichoke hearts, 14-ounce can
❑ Black olives, preferably brine-cured, about 4 ounces
❑ Fresh parsley, 1 small bunch
❑ Fresh basil, 1 small bunch
❑ Red-skinned potatoes, 6 medium, or new potatoes, 18
❑ Fresh chives, 1 small bunch
❑ Breadsticks

MENU

Antipasto, Vegetarian Style

Fresh Italian bread

Serves 6

I love this salad menu, not only because of its ease of preparation and rich diversity, but also because there are several simple, separate components, so that my young sons will actually eat and enjoy many of its parts. Though it is filling as a salad meal in and of itself, you can make a bigger meal by simply cooking some spaghetti and dressing it with your favorite prepared sauce. That makes this a fabulous last-minute meal for company as well.

— N. A.

Strategy:

1. Prepare the antipasto as directed.

2. Warm the Italian bread, if desired, slice it, and arrange it on a platter.

ANTIPASTO, VEGETARIAN STYLE

Don't be daunted by this list of ingredients. Most of them need little, if any, preparation. Most of the work is in simply arranging the ingredients.

3 heaping cups precut broccoli florets
2 heaping cups cauliflower, cut into large florets
2 cups baby carrots
½ cup reduced-fat Italian dressing
1 medium red bell pepper, cut into strips
8 to 12 ounces part-skim or fresh mozzarella, thinly sliced
4 ounces chilled creamy goat cheese

Optional additions (use all or as many as you'd like)
Pepperoncini (marinated hot peppers)
Canned or marinated artichoke hearts
Cherry tomatoes
½ cup (about 4 ounces) oil-cured black olives or pimiento-stuffed green olives

1. Combine the broccoli florets, cauliflower florets, and baby carrots in a large pot with about an inch of water. Cover the pot and steam the vegetables for 4 to 5 minutes, or just until the broccoli is bright green. Drain the vegetables and rinse them under cold water until they're cool.

2. Transfer the vegetables to a shallow container and pour the dressing over them. Let them stand until needed.

3. Prepare the red pepper and cheeses. Arrange the red pepper, cheeses, and whatever optional ingredients you have chosen separately and attractively on a large platter. Just before serving, drain the vegetable mixture (reserve the dressing for another use) and arrange the marinated vegetables on the platter or serve them from a separate bowl. Let everyone serve themselves, taking whatever they wish from the antipasto, along with some fresh Italian bread.

Calories: 260	Total fat: 15 g	Protein: 17 g
Carbohydrate: 12 g	Cholesterol: 44 g	Sodium: 485 mg

Refrigerator staples
- ❏ Pimiento-stuffed green olives (if not using black oil-cured olives)
- ❏ Reduced-fat Italian dressing

Shopping list: fresh foods and nonstaples
- ❏ Precut broccoli florets, about ½ pound
- ❏ Cauliflower, 1 small head
- ❏ Baby carrots, 1 package
- ❏ Red bell pepper, 1 medium
- ❏ Part-skim or fresh mozzarella cheese, 8 to 12 ounces
- ❏ Creamy goat cheese, 4 ounces

Optional ingredients:
- ❏ Pepperoncini (marinated hot peppers), 1 small jar
- ❏ Artichoke hearts, 1 6-ounce jar or 14-ounce can
- ❏ Cherry tomatoes, 1 pint
- ❏ Oil-cured black olives, about 4 ounces (if not using green olives)

Chapter Seven

AMAZINGLY EASY DESSERTS

🕐 🕑 🕒 🕓 🕔

Let's face it — there are times when dessert seems essential. Whether it's because it's a special occasion or just because you want that last lingering taste to be a sweet one, dessert should be a reflection of you and your lifestyle.

Bearing that in mind, we figured that anyone who likes the idea of preparing a full meal in less than 28 minutes would likely not want to spend more than 10 minutes preparing dessert. Here is an assortment of sweet and light endings that take minimal preparation — 5 to 10 minutes, tops. A few do need some additional time to bake or to cool down, during which time you can devote your attention to other things.

In addition to keeping prep time to a minimum, we've also tried to keep fat and sugar content low. Most of these desserts are fruit based and need little or no additional sweetening to make them taste luscious.

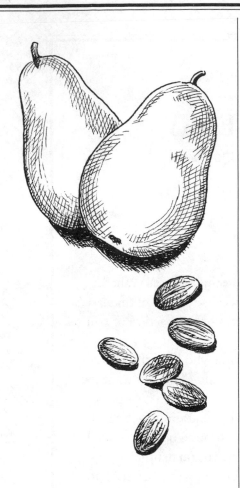

FAST AND FRUITY DESSERT TOPPINGS

BAKED PEARS WITH ALMONDS AND WHEAT GERM

Serves 4 as a topping

4 ripe, sweet pears such as Bosc or Bartlett
⅓ cup plain wheat germ
1 tablespoon light brown sugar
¼ cup sliced almonds
Dash of cinnamon
Low-fat vanilla ice cream, frozen vanilla yogurt, or
 nondairy vanilla frozen dessert

1. Preheat the oven to 400 degrees.

2. Cut the pears into quarters lengthwise, remove the cores and stems, then cut each quarter into thinner slices. Arrange the pears in a small, lightly oiled baking dish.

3. In a small bowl, mix the wheat germ, brown sugar, almonds, and cinnamon. Sprinkle the mixture over the pears.

4. Bake the pears, covered, for 12 to 15 minutes, or until they are tender. Serve warm or at room temperature over low-fat vanilla ice cream, frozen vanilla yogurt, or nondairy vanilla frozen dessert.

Calories: 198	Total fat: 6 g	Protein: 5 g
Carbohydrate: 31 g	Cholesterol: 0 g	Sodium: 3 mg

TIPSY STRAWBERRIES

Serves 4 to 6 as a topping

This works best with really lush, perfectly ripe strawberries.

1 pint fresh, ripe strawberries
3 tablespoons sweet liqueur (Amaretto, Grand Marnier, Cherry Herring, etc.) of your choice
Low-fat vanilla or strawberry ice cream or frozen yogurt, or nondairy vanilla frozen dessert

1. Wash the strawberries, remove their hulls, and cut them into approximately ½-inch dice.

2. Combine the strawberries in a bowl with the liqueur and mix well. Crush about ¼ cup of the strawberries with the tines of a fork and mix again.

3. Cover the strawberry-liqueur mixture and let it stand at least 30 minutes before serving. Serve over low-fat vanilla or strawberry ice cream or frozen yogurt, or nondairy vanilla frozen dessert.

Calories: 55	Total fat: 0 g	Protein: 0 g
Carbohydrate: 8 g	Cholesterol: 0 g	Sodium: 1 mg

FRESH BLUEBERRY SAUCE

Serves 4 to 6 as a topping

1 pint fresh blueberries
¼ cup undiluted frozen apple juice concentrate
1 tablespoon light brown sugar, or to taste (optional)

1. Wash the blueberries. Remove any stems or small leaves.

2. Combine the blueberries in a saucepan with the apple juice. Bring to a simmer, then lower the heat and cook at

a gentle simmer, covered, for 5 minutes. Stir, then simmer uncovered until the blueberries have all burst and the sauce thickens a bit, another 3 to 4 minutes.

3. Taste, and if you'd like the sauce a bit sweeter, add a tablespoon or so of light brown sugar. If the blueberries are ripe and sweet, most likely you will not need any sugar at all. Let the sauce cool, then serve it warm or at room temperature over low-fat vanilla ice cream or frozen yogurt, or nondairy vanilla frozen dessert.

Calories: 45	Total fat: 0 g	Protein: 0 g
Carbohydrate: 11 g	Cholesterol: 0 g	Sodium: 4 mg

PINEAPPLE IN CARAMEL SAUCE

Serves 6

Pineapple with a "burnt" sugar topping is one of the best combinations imaginable.

⅓ cup light brown sugar
⅓ cup juice from pineapple
2 cans pineapple slices in natural juices, drained, juices reserved
1½ cups low-fat vanilla yogurt

1. In a small heavy saucepan, combine the sugar and 3 tablespoons of water. Cook over medium heat, stirring, until the sugar dissolves. Bring it to a boil and cook without stirring until the sugar turns a rich golden brown, about 5 minutes. Be careful not to allow it to get too brown or it will taste burned.

2. Remove the pan from the heat and stir the pineapple juice in slowly. Return the pan to the heat. Cook over low heat until the caramel is smooth and melted into the juice.

3. Arrange two slices of pineapple in each dish and top with the caramel sauce, then with about a ¼-cup scoop of the yogurt, and serve.

| Calories: 220 | Total fat: 3 g | Protein: 11 g |
| Carbohydrate: 36 g | Cholesterol: 12 g | Sodium: 138 mg |

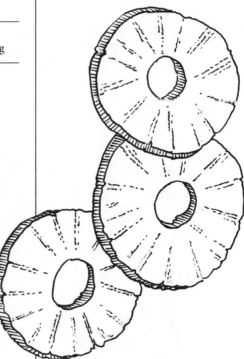

PIÑA COLADA BANANA COUPÉ

Serves 6

1-pound can pineapple chunks in natural juices
⅓ cup shredded unsweetened coconut
2 tablespoons honey or brown rice syrup
½ cup crumbled soft or silken tofu
2 small ripe, firm bananas, peeled and sliced

Garnishes (use one or both, optional)
1 ripe kiwi, peeled and sliced
Shredded coconut

1. In a blender or food processor fitted with a steel blade, puree the pineapple, coconut, honey or rice syrup, and tofu until quite smooth.

2. Divide the banana slices among 6 pudding cups (or stemmed wineglasses), cover them with the pineapple mixture, and, if desired, top with slices of kiwi and a sprinkling of shredded coconut. Serve immediately, or chill for an hour or so before serving.

| Calories: 191 | Total fat: 9 g | Protein: 3 g |
| Carbohydrate: 26 g | Cholesterol: 0 g | Sodium: 8 mg |

PINEAPPLE-YOGURT AMBROSIA

Serves 6

This refreshing dessert is particularly pleasing after a spicy meal.

1-pound can unsweetened pineapple chunks, drained, juice reserved for another use
1-pound container vanilla low-fat yogurt
¼ cup dark raisins
2 small seedless oranges, peeled and sectioned

1. Combine all of the ingredients in a serving dish and stir well. Chill until needed or serve at once in dessert cups.

Calories: 186	Total fat: 1 g	Protein: 6 g
Carbohydrate: 37 g	Cholesterol: 5 g	Sodium: 69 mg

FLAME GRAPES BRÛLÉE

Serves 8

This is yet another dramatic presentation that takes only a few minutes to prepare, with crisp, sweet seedless red grapes hiding under a blanket of sour cream and topped with a crunchy brown sugar topping.

1 pound red (sometimes called Flame) seedless grapes, washed and stemmed
2 cups low-fat (not fat-free) sour cream
⅓ cup dark brown sugar
½ cup honey-sweetened wheat germ

1. Preheat the broiler.

2. Arrange the grapes in a 7- by 11-inch baking or oval

gratin dish. Spoon the sour cream over the top. In a small bowl, combine the brown sugar and wheat germ. Sprinkle the sugar mixture evenly over the sour cream.

3. Slide the dish under the broiler and broil, watching carefully, until the sugar starts bubbling and becomes caramelized, 3 to 5 minutes. Be sure to cool for 5 or 10 minutes before serving; hot sugar can give a nasty burn!

Calories: 175	Total fat: 8 g	Protein: 4 g
Carbohydrate: 20 g	Cholesterol: 4 g	Sodium: 27 mg

APPLES WITH TAFFY CREAM

Serves 6

8-ounce package soft, low-fat cream cheese (Neufchâtel)
⅓ cup honey or maple syrup
1 tablespoon vanilla extract
½ cup chopped peanuts (optional)
6 medium sweet, crisp apples
Juice of ½ lemon

1. In a small bowl, combine the cream cheese, honey or syrup, and vanilla. Beat the mixture with a spoon until it's smooth and well-blended. Scatter the nuts on top, if desired.

2. Just before serving, peel the apples, then quarter them and remove the cores. Cut each quarter into two slices. As they are cut, put the slices into a medium-sized mixing bowl filled with water, combined with the lemon juice, to prevent darkening.

3. When all the slices are done, arrange them on a platter and place the bowl of taffy cream in the center for dipping.

Calories: 243	Total fat: 9 g	Protein: 4 g
Carbohydrate: 35 g	Cholesterol: 33 g	Sodium: 155 mg

POACHED PEARS WITH GINGER NUT CRUMBLES

Serves 6

Crunchy nuts and cookie crumbles over tender poached pears is a great company dessert in the fall, when pears are both plentiful and relatively inexpensive.

2 tablespoons lemon juice
1 cup white grape juice (bottled or reconstituted from
    frozen concentrate)
1 tablespoon butter or soy margarine, cut into bits
3 tablespoons honey
¼ teaspoon ground cinnamon
6 small ripe but firm Bosc or Anjou pears
¾ cup crushed gingersnap cookies
¼ cup finely chopped walnuts

1. In a large, heavy saucepan, combine the lemon juice, grape juice, butter or margarine, honey, and cinnamon. Bring to a boil, lower the heat, and simmer for 3 minutes.

2. With a vegetable peeler, peel the pears, leaving them whole and the stems intact on top. As each is peeled, lower it into the hot, barely simmering syrup. Cover the pears and poach them for 10 minutes, then remove the saucepan from the heat.

3. Remove the pears from the syrup and set on a plate to cool, reserving the syrup. When the pears are cool enough

to handle, scoop out the core from each, starting at the bottom end, with a melon baller or a sharp paring knife.

4. To serve, place a pear in each serving bowl, stem pointing up, divide the syrup among them, and sprinkle each generously with the crushed gingersnaps and nuts. Serve warm or at room temperature.

Calories: 252	Total fat: 6 g	Protein: 2 g
Carbohydrate: 46 g	Cholesterol: 0 g	Sodium: 100 mg

BAKED BANANAS

This is a sublime way to use up overripe bananas. When baked, bananas become super sweet, with the consistency of pudding.

1 very ripe or overripe banana per person
Vanilla yogurt or frozen yogurt
Fresh berries (use whole raspberries, blueberries, or chopped strawberries)

1. Preheat the oven to 400 degrees.

2. Make a lengthwise slit in the peel of each banana, then arrange, unpeeled, on a foil-lined baking sheet.

3. Bake the bananas for 10 minutes, or until the peels are completely black and the juices are running.

4. Arrange each banana on a plate and split the peel open. Top with a scoop of vanilla yogurt and a handful of fresh berries.

Calories: 141	Total fat: 0 g	Protein: 3 g
Carbohydrate: 31 g	Cholesterol: 2 g	Sodium: 22 mg

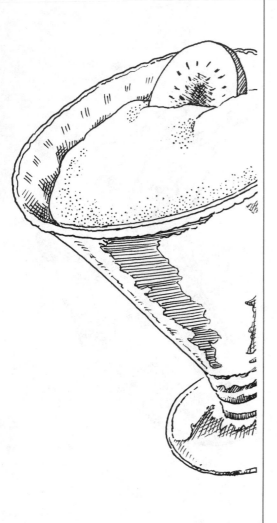

QUICK SILKEN TOFU CHOCOLATE PUDDING

Serves 8

Here's a luscious pudding that can be made minus the bother of cooking and thickening a liquid. And it's dairy-free, too. Silken tofu, which comes in 10-ounce aseptic-packed boxes, is available in most natural food stores, and many supermarkets now carry it, too.

6 ounces semisweet chocolate chips
2 10-ounce packages firm silken (aseptic-packed) tofu
1 to 2 tablespoons brown sugar, honey, or brown rice
    syrup, or to taste
Dash of nutmeg

1. Melt the chocolate chips in a small saucepan or double boiler with a tablespoon of water over medium heat.

2. Transfer the melted chocolate to the container of a food processor fitted with a steel blade. Add the tofu and process until smooth. Add the brown sugar, honey, or rice syrup to taste, and sprinkle in the nutmeg. Process again until velvety smooth.

3. Divide the pudding among 6 dessert cups and chill until needed.

Variation: Stir some sliced banana into the pudding, and/or top with some slices of kiwifruit.

Calories: 157	Total fat: 8 g	Protein: 6 g
Carbohydrate: 14 g	Cholesterol: 0 g	Sodium: 37 mg

PEACH MELBA YOGURT WITH STRAWBERRY-RASPBERRY PUREE

Serves 4

Strawberries and raspberries combined in a puree, known as melba sauce, is a French classic. Somehow the combination heightens the flavors of both fruits.

½ pint fresh, sweet strawberries, washed
1 cup fresh raspberries, washed
2 tablespoons undiluted apple juice concentrate, or to taste
4 fresh peaches, washed and sliced
2 8-ounce containers low-fat peach yogurt, well-stirred, or 1 pint low-fat frozen peach yogurt

1. Remove the hulls from the strawberries, then combine them in a food processor or blender with the raspberries. Process just until well pureed but not liquefied.

2. Force the puree through a fine sieve into a small mixing bowl. Stir in the apple juice concentrate, sweetening the sauce to taste.

3. Divide the sliced peaches among 4 dessert cups. Top with ½ cup of peach yogurt, then the sauce. Serve at once.

Calories: 208	Total fat: 2 g	Protein: 6 g
Carbohydrate: 37 g	Cholesterol: 5 g	Sodium: 65 mg

INDEX